NEXT-DAY
JOB INTERVIEW

prepare tonight and get the job tomorrow

Second Edition

MICHAEL FARR and DICK GAITHER

jist
Works
America's Career Publisher

NEXT-DAY JOB INTERVIEW, SECOND EDITION

© 2009 by JIST Publishing

Published by JIST Works, an imprint of JIST Publishing
7321 Shadeland Station, Suite 200
Indianapolis, IN 46256-3923
Phone: 800-648-JIST
E-mail: info@jist.com

Fax: 877-454-7839
Web site: www.jist.com

See the back of this book for additional JIST titles and ordering information. Quantity discounts are available for JIST books. Have future editions of JIST books automatically delivered to you on publication through our convenient standing order program. Please call our Sales Department at 800-648-JIST (5478) for a free catalog and more information.

Acquisitions Editor: Lori Cates Hand
Project Editor: Aaron Black
Interior Designer: Aleata Halbig
Page Layout: Toi Davis
Cover Designers: Katy Bodenmiller, Alan Evans
Proofreaders: Paula Lowell, Jeanne Clark
Indexer: Kelly D. Henthorne

Printed in the United States of America
13 12 11 10 09   9 8 7 6 5 4 3 2

    Library of Congress Cataloging-in-Publication data

Farr, J. Michael
    Next-day job interview : prepare tonight and get the job tomorrow / Michael Farr and
    Dick Gaither. -- 2nd ed.
        p. cm.
    Includes index.
    ISBN 978-1-59357-604-2 (alk. paper)
    1. Employment interviewing. 2. Job hunting. I. Gaither, Richard. II. Title.
    HF5549.5.I6F368 2009
    650.14'4--dc22
                        2008031788

We have been careful to provide accurate information in this book, but it is possible that errors and omissions have been introduced. Please consider this in making any career plans or other important decisions. Trust your own judgment above all else and in all things.

Trademarks: All brand names and product names used in this book are trade names, service marks, trademarks, or registered trademarks of their respective owners.

ISBN 978-1-59357-604-2

This Short, Small Book Can Make a Big Difference

The interview is the single most important activity in a job search. So, when you're preparing for the interview, you need to understand one of the most basic and universal rules of job seeking:

The people who get the job offers might not be the best qualified people, but they are the people who interview the best.

The information presented in this book is designed to help you become one of those people who interview the best. Here are a few things to think about as you prepare yourself for an interview.

Getting an interview makes you special. If an employer calls you in for an interview, there are three assumptions you can make about yourself, the employer, and your job search:

- The information in your resume, cover letter, and application form met the employer's basic hiring criteria.

- You've just beat out 80 percent of the competition. You're one of the top five or six candidates still in the running for the job.

- The interviewer is seriously considering you for employment and is giving you a chance to convince him or her that you're the right person for the job.

Interviewing is a learned skill. Very few people are "naturally" good interviewees. What transforms a person from an interviewee into someone who gets the job can be summed up with the following five phrases:

- Good interviewees understand the interview process and have anticipated the questions they will be asked.

- Good interviewees have researched the company, the job demands, the field, and the interviewer, and use that information to their advantage during interviews.

- Good interviewees have a thorough knowledge of what they can offer an employer, what they want from employers, and what sets them apart from the competition.

- Good interviewees have invested time and energy in building powerful interview responses, and they practice answering common interview questions.

- Good interviewees are persistent. They follow up after interviews, send thank-you notes, and refuse to accept rejection without learning something from it.

The information, exercises, and activities in this book address each of the preceding points.

Interviewing requires persuasive communication skills. The information in this book will help you verbally convince the interviewer that you are a better hiring risk, that you're a good fit with your coworkers, and that you will bring more to the company than your competition would.

Interviewing is a fear-provoking activity. Most interview fear stems from two sources:

- Insufficient knowledge about what to do and how to do it

- A lack of practice

By learning what employers expect from you and practicing your answers, you can eliminate much of your interview fear and anxiety.

Reducing interview mistakes results in more job offers. As in any competition, the player who makes the fewest mistakes usually wins the game. This book points out the most common interview mistakes and shows you how to eliminate them and win the game.

Interview perfection is unattainable. You don't have to be a perfect interviewee. You just need to be better than your competition and beat them by one point. Working through this book will help you gain an advantage over applicants who didn't invest the time to prepare that you have.

Now it's time to get to work improving your interview skills and building your interview poise and confidence level!

Table of Contents

A Brief Introduction to Using This Book

Ideally, the best way to prepare for an interview is to research the organization and the job for a week or two, get a good handle on your qualifications and experience, and carefully consider your responses to the tough questions that might come up. But you have an interview tomorrow that was just offered to you today or that you were too busy to prepare for before now. How can you get up to speed tonight?

What's in This Book

1. **Read some quick tips to dramatically improve your performance.**
   The tips in chapter 1 will quickly help you improve your interviewing skills—enough to get through an interview later today or tomorrow. They provide a short but thorough interviewing course and will teach you far more than most of your competitors know about interviewing.

2. **Know thyself.** Use the worksheets in chapter 2 to quantify what you can do so that you can present yourself well to the interviewer.

3. **Get the inside scoop.** Chapter 3 shows you some quick ways to find information about the job and the organization that will come in handy during the interview.

4. **Know how to answer the key interview questions.** Chapter 4 shows you a process for answering most interview questions and then guides you through using it to create solid answers to 10 frequently asked problem questions.

5. **Be ready to handle unusual questions in a positive way.** Chapter 5 gives advice on handling difficult questions about your personal situation and convincing an employer why you should be hired over someone else.

6. **Close the interview correctly.** Chapter 6 gives tips on how to wrap things up and make a lasting positive impression on your interviewer.

7. **Follow up.** Often the key to turning interviews into offers is following up effectively. Chapter 7 shows you how to keep yourself foremost in the interviewer's mind.

8. **Negotiate your salary.** The interview went well and you've been offered the job! But how can you be sure you're getting the salary you're worth? Chapter 8 gives you insights on how to handle this stressful phase of the interview process.

There's no need to read these chapters in order; just spend time on what you think offers the biggest payoff for you and where you need the most help.

Are You Ready for an Interview?

Sometimes it's not what you don't know that gets you in trouble. It's what you think you know that isn't really true that causes the most trouble. This is especially true of the interview process. I've rarely met anyone who admits to being a rotten interviewee, even after they've been rejected. So let's see what you really know about yourself and the interview process.

There's an old adage:

If you're going to run with the big dogs, you have to get off the porch.

Evaluate your interview success readiness by completing this simple quiz to see whether you're almost ready to run with the big dogs at the interview or whether you're sitting on the porch with the puppies.

1. Can you talk the talk of the industry, using buzzwords, jargon, and acronyms that are common to the industry?

   Yes   No

2. Can you give the interviewer at least three reasons why you're interested in his or her company?

   Yes   No

3. Can you list 15 common interview mistakes?

   Yes   No

4. Can you readily give at least three examples of times when you did work that wasn't included in your job description?

   Yes   No

5. Can you identify three prominent employment-related successes or achievements you've had and talk about your role in them?

   Yes   No

6. Can you comfortably give the interviewer at least five good reasons why his or her company should hire you?

               Yes   **No**

7. Do you have a 60-second promotional presentation ready to respond to the question, "Can you tell me a little about yourself?"

               Yes   **No**

8. Do you have a job description for the position and are you able to give three examples of when you've used each skill and strength listed in it?

               Yes   **No**

9. Are you confident that you can answer technical questions interviewers ask or pass an employment test?

               Yes   **No**

10. Have you researched the pay scale and benefits packages for people with your skills and experience working in similar positions in your locale?

               Yes   **No**

11. Have you anticipated 10 questions you'll be asked at the interview and made notes about how you'll answer them?

               Yes   **No**

12. Do you have a rational and acceptable set of reasons for leaving, or wanting to leave, your last job?

               Yes   **No**

13. Have you practiced negotiating a higher salary and answering the pay expectations question?

               Yes   **No**

14. Do you understand the interview methods, styles, and protocols for your particular industry?

               Yes   **No**

15. Can you list 15 of your marketable skills, abilities, and personality traits that make you a good hiring risk?

    Yes   No

16. If the interviewer asks you to take a drug test "right now," would you be willing to do so and would you pass it?

    Yes   No

17. Have you researched the company and can you comfortably talk about its products, services, goals, and competitors?

    Yes   No

18. Will you immediately follow up after the interview with a thank-you note, letter, or e-mail ?

    Yes   No

19. Do you have a list of at least five intelligent questions you want to have answered at the interview? (Questions about pay and benefits don't count!)

    Yes   No

20. Do you have a business card that highlights your achievements to leave with interviewers at the end of the interview?

    Yes   No

So how do you measure up? Count your number of NO responses and see the following chart.

15–21 NOs	You're on the porch with the puppies! Use this book to get through tomorrow's interview and seek outside help in further improving your interview skills in the future.
8–14 NOs	You're average. But remember, average isn't acceptable in an interview. This book will make you great.

| 1–7 NOs | You're running with the big dogs. At this level, the competition is fierce. Use this book to improve your odds of being leader of the pack. |

So what are you waiting for? Jump right in and start improving your interview skills right now!

Chapter 1

Quick and Essential Tips for Tomorrow's Interview

The interview is the most important 60 minutes of any job search. A great deal is at stake, yet research indicates that most people are not well-prepared for the interview process. This lack of preparation can be good news for you, because reading this book can help you substantially improve your interviewing skills, thereby giving you an advantage over the majority of job seekers. We have seen many employers hire people who present themselves well in an interview instead of others with superior credentials.

This chapter is based on substantial research into how employers decide on hiring one person over another. Although the interview itself is an incredibly complex interaction, we have found that there are simple things you can do that make a big difference in getting a job offer. This chapter presents some of the tricks we have learned over the years.

Eight Common Interview Formats

Before we get into the specifics of how to succeed in interviews, it might help you to read about some of the different forms your interview might take. There are a bundle of different interviewing formats that employers use to ferret out information, but you'd go into retirement preparing to deal with every one of them. Because of this, our focus will be on discussing the most common interview formats you're likely to be exposed to.

The Preliminary Screening Interview

Usually in the first interview, you meet with a person whose role is to screen applicants and arrange follow-up interviews with the person who has the authority to hire. Other times, you might meet directly with the hiring authority, whose primary focus is to eliminate as many applicants as possible, leaving only one or two. The focus of the techniques presented in this chapter is on these one-on-one interviews.

The Panel Interview

Although still not as common as the one-on-one interview, this interview format is gaining in popularity. You interview with two or more people involved in the selection process or people who might be your coworkers or supervisors. In this format, you'll likely be hit with interview questions suited to several different types of interviews: technical, situational, behavioral, and interpersonal.

An extension of the panel interview is the group interview. In this situation, one or more interviewers meet with a group of applicants, all in the room at the same time, so that the interviewers can observe the interpersonal and leadership traits of the people in the group. The techniques used in this book work well in these settings, too.

The Stress Interview

Some interviewers intentionally try to get you upset. They want to see how you handle stress, whether you can accept criticism, or how you react to a tense situation. They hope to see how you are likely to act in a high-pressure job.

For example, an interviewer using this method might try to upset you by not accepting something you say as true. "I find it difficult to believe," this person might say, "that you were responsible for as large a program as you claim here on your resume. Why don't you just tell me what you really did?" Another approach is to quickly fire questions at you, but not give you time to completely answer, or to interrupt you mid-sentence with other questions.

I hope you don't run into this sort of interview; but if you do, be yourself and have a few laughs. The odds are the interview could turn out fine if you don't take the bait. Don't get emotional, become anxious, or act unsettled while answering the questions. If you do get a job offer following such an interview, you might want to ask yourself whether you would want to work for such a person or organization. Politely turn down the job if you decide against the position. You never know when you might encounter that interviewer again, given that he or she works in your industry.

The Structured (Competency-Based) Interview

Employment laws related to hiring practices have increased the use of structured interviews, particularly in larger organizations. In this type of interview, the interviewer has a list of questions to ask all applicants and a form to fill out to record the responses and observations. Your experience and skills might be compared to specific job tasks or criteria. Even with such a highly structured interview, you will likely have an opportunity to present what you feel is essential information.

The Behavioral Interview

Even though some of the more traditional questions might be asked like, "What is the best way to handle customer complaints," and "Can you tell me about yourself?" the focus of this interview method is to ask for examples of situations in which you displayed certain characteristics or handled certain issues. A behavioral interview question usually sounds like this: "Can you give me an example of a time when, or tell me about a specific situation in which, you handled a customer complaint?"

Some folks call this the "storytelling" interview format because interviewers are looking for the who, what, where, when, why, and how in a story about a sought-after trait or ability. The story should include quantifiable, measurable, and positive results, and it should define how the example relates (links) to the new position. The Prove It technique used throughout this book is especially powerful in a behavioral interview.

The Social Interview

This is the worst type of interview format you can run into in terms of having a chance to well represent yourself and your abilities. It's one of the few times when you really have to take total control of the process. You will come across many inexperienced interviewers who will not do a good job of interviewing you. They might talk about themselves too much or neglect to ask you meaningful questions. Many employers are competent managers but poor interviewers, and few have had any formal interview training. The best way to handle this type of interview is to present the interviewer with the skills you have to do this job—even if he or she doesn't ask.

The Unstructured Interview

A relative of the social interview is the unstructured interview. In this format, the interviewer might have a list of preplanned questions to ask in a specific order but tends to "go with the flow." You can count on having a lot of follow-up questions based on your initial interview response, and don't be surprised if you end up fielding some illegal questions with this format.

The Technical Interview

With this format, you have one or more people who are highly proficient in the job verbally testing you by asking job-specific questions. If you can't answer the questions correctly, you're done for. There's not much this book can do to help you with this type of interview except advise you to get your hands on some tests commonly used in your career field and have someone quiz you to see where you need the most brushing up.

Eleven Important Actions for Interview Success

Interview success depends on three factors:

- Knowing yourself and what you have to offer the employer.

- What you know about the employer, the field, and the company.

- How you present that information in the pressure-cooker environment called the interview.

The following 11 actions, compiled with these factors in mind, are critical to setting yourself apart from the competition and generating a job offer.

Although most people know that the interview is important to both you and the employer, few job seekers have a clear sense of what they need to accomplish during those critical minutes. Later chapters describe interview techniques in more detail, but what follows will help you get a quick understanding of the most important actions to take in an interview.

Make a Positive Impression

You only have seven seconds to make a first impression. Employers rarely hire someone who makes a negative first (or later) impression. These tips can help you make a positive impression before and during your interview.

Before the Interview

What happens before the interview is extremely important, although it's often overlooked. Before you meet prospective employers, you often have indirect contact with those who know them. You might even contact the employer directly through e-mail, a phone call, or other correspondence. Each of these contacts creates an impression. There are three ways an interviewer might form an impression of you before meeting you face-to-face:

- **The interviewer already knows you.** An employer might know you as a friend or former coworker or through a mutual acquaintance. In this situation, your best approach is to acknowledge that relationship, but treat the interview in all other respects as a business meeting.

- **You have contacted the interviewer through e-mail or by phone.** E-mail and the phone are important job search tools. How you handle these contact points creates an impression, even though the contacts are brief. For example, both contact via the phone and contact via e-mail give an impression of your language skills and ability to present yourself in a competent way; e-mail also quickly communicates your level of written communication skills. So if you set up an interview with the employer by contacting him or her directly through phone or e-mail, you have already created an impression.

  You should call the day before the interview to verify the time of your meeting. Say something like, "Hi, I want to confirm our interview for two o'clock tomorrow." Get any directions you need. This kind of call demonstrates your attention to detail and helps to communicate the importance you place on this interview.

  > **Tip:** *Administrative assistants, receptionists, and other staff you have contact with will mention their observations of you to the interviewer, so be professional and courteous in all encounters with staff.*

- **The interviewer has read your resume and other job search correspondence.** Prior to most interviews, you provide the employer with some sort of information or paperwork that creates an impression. Sending a note, letter, or e-mail beforehand often creates the impression that you are well-organized. Applications, resumes, and other correspondence sent or e-mailed in advance help the interviewer know more about you. If such correspondence is well done, it will help to create a positive impression. (For quick advice on putting together an effective resume, see *Same-Day Resume,* another book in the *Help in a Hurry* series.)

The Day of the Interview

To make a good impression on interview day, use these tips:

- **Get there on time.** Try to schedule several interviews within the same area of town and time frame to avoid wasting time on excessive travel. Get directions online (from www.mapquest.com or a similar source) or ask for directions from the target company's receptionist to be sure you know how to get to the interview and how long traveling to the interview will take. Allow plenty of time for traffic or other problems and plan on arriving for the interview 5 to 10 minutes early.

- **Check your appearance.** Arrive early enough to slip into a restroom and correct any grooming problems your travel might have caused, such as wind-blown hair. You would be surprised how many people go into the interview with messed-up hair or smudged lipstick on their teeth. Use a breath mint or gum just to be on the safe side. Do not spray on perfume, cologne, or hairspray right before the interview because many people are sensitive to chemicals and scents.

- **Use appropriate waiting-room behavior.** As you wait for the interview to begin, keep in mind that it's important to relax and to look relaxed. Occupy yourself with something businesslike. For example, you could review your notes on questions you might like to ask in the interview, key skills you want to present, or other interview details. Bring a work-related magazine to read or pick up one in the reception area. The waiting room might also have publications from the organization itself that you might not have seen yet. You could also use this time to update your daily schedule.

  Tip: *Identify things you habitually do that might create a negative impression and avoid doing them during the interview. For example, don't slouch, crack your knuckles, mess with your hair, or spread your papers across the next seat. Do not smoke.*

- **Be prepared if the interviewer is late.** Hope that it happens. If you arrive promptly but have to wait past the appointed time, that puts the interviewer in a "Gee, I'm sorry, I owe you one" frame of mind. If the interviewer is 15 minutes late, approach the office manager or administrative assistant and say something like:

"I have another appointment to keep today. Do you think it will be much longer before [insert interviewer's name] will be free?" Be nice, but don't act as though you can sit around all day, either. If you have to wait more than 25 minutes beyond the scheduled time, you might want to ask to reschedule the interview at a better time. Say it is no problem for you and you understand things do come up. Besides, you'll say, you want to be sure Mr. or Ms. So-and-So doesn't feel rushed when he or she sees you. Set up the new time, accept any apology with a smile, and go on your way. When you do come back for your interview, the odds are that the interviewer will apologize—and treat you very well indeed.

- **Be particular about your dress and appearance.** How you dress and groom can create a big negative or positive impression, especially during the first few seconds of an interview. With so many options in styles, colors, and other factors, determining the correct approach can get quite complex. To avoid the complexity, follow this simple rule: Dress and groom the way the interviewer is likely to be dressed and groomed, but just a bit better.

- **Give a firm handshake, maintain good eye contact, show some energy, and smile.** This is called creating chemistry. Having a pulse (energy) and a smile when you meet the interviewer are worth five points. If the employer offers his or her hand, give a firm (but not too firm) handshake as you smile. As ridiculous as it sounds, a little practice helps. Avoid staring, but do look at the interviewer when either of you is speaking. It will help you concentrate on what is being said and indicate to the employer that you are listening closely and have good social skills.

- **Pay attention to body language.** Good interviewers don't just listen to your answers; they watch your body to see if it's saying the same thing your mouth is. Don't slouch. Exhibit interest by leaning slightly forward in your chair, and keep your head up, looking directly at the interviewer. Avoid the fidgets, such as straightening your clothes, brushing your hair, and messing with your jewelry. Don't cross your arms across your chest. Even though not absolutely true, many people see this as a sign of resistance.

- **Eliminate annoying verbal behaviors.** We've all got them! Saying "aaahhh" or "ummmmm" frequently, or saying "you know what I mean?" over and over, or using other repetitive words or phrases is like fingernails on a blackboard for the interviewer. You might hardly be aware of doing this, but do watch for it. Ask friends or family for help pinpointing these behaviors.

- **Pay attention to your voice.** If you are naturally soft-spoken, work on increasing your volume slightly. Listen to news announcers and other professional speakers who are good models for volume, speed, and voice tone. Your confidence and poise on the job are judged by how you come across during the interview. At-home practice and going to more interviews is the only way your voice and delivery will improve.

- **Use the interviewer's formal name and title often.** Do this particularly in the early part of the interview and again when you are ending it. Do not call the interviewer by his or her first name unless the interviewer suggests that you should. If he or she has a title (Sgt. _____, Dr. _____, etc.), use it.

- **Get ready for a little small talk—but not too much.** A brief amount of interview time is allotted to putting applicants at ease. Be friendly and make a few appropriate comments. You need to walk a little bit of a razor's edge between being social and pushing your agenda of presenting positive information about your skills, abilities, and experiences.

- **Ask some opening questions.** As soon as you have completed the necessary pleasant chitchat, be prepared to guide the interview in the direction you want the interview to go. This process can happen within a minute of your first greeting, but is more likely to take up to five minutes. See "Use Control Statements to Your Advantage" later in this chapter for details on how to do this.

Communicate Your Most Marketable Skills

You enter the interview with three sets of skills desired by employers: job-related, self-management, and transferable. Each tells the interviewer something different about you. Be prepared to talk about what you can offer an employer. The most successful interviewees can present three examples of each of their skills and show how those skills meet an employer's needs. If you have created a reasonably positive image of yourself, an interviewer will next be interested in the specifics of why he or she should consider hiring you. The back-and-forth conversation probing your skill sets and talents usually lasts from 15 to 45 minutes. Many consider it to be the most important—and most difficult—task in the entire job search.

The only thing you have to do is to communicate your skills by directly and completely answering the questions an employer asks you. Chapter 2 helps you recognize your skills so that you can communicate them to an interviewer.

Use Control Statements to Your Advantage

A *control statement* is a statement you make that becomes the roadmap for where the rest of the conversation is going. Although you might think you are at the mercy of the interviewer, you do have some ability to set the direction of the interview.

For example, you might say something direct, such as "I'd like to tell you about what I've done, what I enjoy doing, and why I think I would be a good match with your organization." Your control statement can come at the beginning of the interview if things seem fuzzy after the chitchat or at any time in the interview when you feel the focus is shifting away from the points you want to make.

Here are some other control statements and questions to ask early in an interview:

- "I know that right now your company needs a strong 'rainmaker' to generate new sales. Could we spend some time talking about how I can fill this need for you?"

- "I have some insights on how your competition is overcoming the same obstacles that you face. Would you like me to share them?"

- "May I share with you my personal philosophy for success?"

Anticipate the Types of Questions You'll Be Asked

According to a recent survey by the Society for Human Resource Management, how a person responds to interview questions is viewed as the single most important factor in making hiring decisions, above education and experience. So anticipating the questions you will be asked during interviews is crucial to your success.

You should also try to anticipate questions that might address concerns the interviewer has—such as lack of education and experience or resume gaps—and present powerful counters to those concerns. You'll find these dealt with in chapter 5.

Ask Good Questions

At some point in the interview, most employers ask whether you have any questions. The types of questions you ask—and when you ask them—affect the interviewer's evaluation of you. So be prepared to ask insightful questions about the organization. One formula for interview failure is No Questions = No Interest = No Job Offer!

Good topics to touch on include the following:

- How the organization is fairing against its competition
- Executive management styles
- What obstacles the organization anticipates in meeting its goals
- How the organization's goals have changed over the past three years

Generally, asking about pay, benefits, or other similar topics at this time is unwise. The reason is that doing so tends to make you seem more interested in what the organization can do for you, rather than in what you can do for it.

Help Employers Know Why They Should Hire You

Even if the interviewer never directly says it, the question on his or her mind is always "Why should I hire you over someone else?" The best response to this question highlights advantages you offer to the employer, not advantages that they offer to you. A good response provides proof that you can help an employer make more money by improving efficiency, reducing costs, increasing sales, or solving problems. See chapter 4 for further guidance on answering this all-important question.

Close the Interview Properly

As the interview comes to a close, it's your job to leave a lasting impression, not just a good first one. To do this, you need to

- **Summarize the key points of the interview.** Use your judgment here and keep it short! Review the major issues that came up during the interview. You can skip this step if time is short.
- **If a problem came up, repeat your resolution of it.** Whatever you think that particular interviewer might see as a reason not to hire you, bring it up again and present the reasons why you don't see it as a

problem. If you are not sure what the interviewer is thinking, be direct and ask, "Is there anything about me that concerns you or might keep you from hiring me?" Whatever comes up, do as well as you can in responding to it. And don't act frazzled by the possibility or presence of a problem. Just solve it.

- **Review your strengths for this job.** Take this opportunity to one more time present the skills you possess that relate to this particular job. Emphasize only your key strengths and keep your statements brief.

- **If you want the job, ask for it.** If you want the job, say so and explain why. Employers are more willing to hire someone they know is excited about a job, so let them know if you are excited. If it seems appropriate, ask when you can start.

Be Ready to Negotiate

Don't always go for the first offer, even if you need the job badly. Contrary to what you might think, employers expect some level of negotiation (salary, benefits, duties, hours, and so on). Virtually everything is negotiable, and once an employer sends you the message that they want you, your ability to negotiate elevates.

Be Competitive...with Style

Interviewers say that the heart of interview success is aggressively showing the interviewer that you can do the job, exceed the job responsibilities, and want the job. But this aggressive behavior must be tempered with a little style and class so that you don't just come off as a blowhard or overconfident showman.

Follow Up After the Interview

The interview has ended, you made it home, and now you just sit back and wait, right? Wrong. Effective follow-up actions can make a big difference in getting a job offer.

As we say throughout this book, following up can make the difference in getting the job you want fast. See chapter 7 for more details on effective follow-up by phone, e-mail, and regular mail.

Use a Three-Step Process for Answering Most Interview Questions

There are thousands of questions that you could be asked in an interview, and there is no way you can memorize a "correct" response for each one— especially not tonight before the interview. Interviews just aren't like that, because they are often conversational and informal. The unexpected happens. For these reasons, developing an approach to answering an interview question is far more important than memorizing a canned response.

You can use a technique called the Three-Step Process to fashion an effective answer to most interview questions.

Step 1: Understand What Is Really Being Asked

Most questions relate to your ability to adapt and your personality. These questions include "Can we depend on you?" "Are you easy to get along with?" and "Are you a good worker?" The question might also relate to whether you have the experience and training to do the job if you are hired.

Remember that employers often hire the people who present themselves well in an interview over those with better credentials. Your best shot is to emphasize whatever personal strengths you have that could offer an advantage to an employer. The person might ask for a time when you handled a customer complaint, but what he or she wants to know is whether you have anything going for you that can help you handle situations better than another worker.

Well, do you? Are you a hard worker? Do you learn fast? Have you had intensive training or hands-on experience? Do you have skills from other activities that can transfer to this job? Knowing in advance what skills you have to offer is essential to answering interview questions correctly.

Step 2: Answer the Question Briefly in a Nondamaging Way

A good response to a question should acknowledge the facts of your situation and present them as an advantage rather than a disadvantage. For example, the following response answers the question asked without hurting your chances of getting the job:

Question: "We were looking for someone with more experience in this field than you seem to have. Why should we consider you over others with better credentials?"

Answer: "I'm sure there are people who have more years of experience or better credentials. I do, however, have four years of combined training and hands-on experience using the latest methods and techniques. Because my training is recent, I am open to new ideas and am used to working hard and learning quickly."

Step 3: Answer the Real Question by Presenting Your Related Skills

An effective response to any interview question should answer the question in a direct way that also presents your ability to do the job well. Although the response in step 2 answered the question in an appropriate and brief way, you might continue with additional details that emphasize key skills needed for the job:

> "As you know, I held down a full-time job and family responsibilities while going to school. During those two years, I had an excellent attendance record both at work and school, missing only one day in two years. I also received two merit increases in salary, and my grades were in the top 25 percent of my class. In order to do all this, I had to learn to organize my time and set priorities. I worked hard to prepare myself in this new career area and am willing to keep working to establish myself. The position you have available is what I am prepared to do. I am willing to work harder than the next person because I have the desire to keep learning and to do an outstanding job. With my education complete, I can now turn my full attention to this job."

That response presents the skills necessary to do well in any job. The job seeker sounds dependable. She also gave examples of situations where she had used the required skills in other settings.

Chapter 4 shows you how to use the Three-Step Process to provide thorough answers to interview questions that, in one form or another, are asked in most interviews. If you can answer those questions well, you should be prepared to answer almost any question.

The Prove It Technique

The Three-Step Process is important for understanding that the interview question being asked is often an attempt to discover underlying information. You can further provide that information effectively by using the Prove It technique:

1. **Present a concrete example.** People relate to and remember stories. Saying you have a skill is not nearly as powerful as describing a situation where you used that skill. The example should include enough details to make sense of the who, what, where, when, how, and why.

2. **Quantify.** Whenever possible, use numbers to provide a basis for what you did. For example, give the number of customers served, the percent you exceeded quotas, dollar amounts you were responsible for, or the number of new accounts you generated.

3. **Emphasize results.** Providing some data regarding the positive results you obtained is important. For example, you could state that sales increased by 3 percent over the preceding year or profits went up 50 percent. Use numbers to quantify your results.

4. **Link it up.** Although the connection between your example and doing the job well might seem obvious to you, make sure it is clear to the employer. A simple statement is often enough to accomplish this.

If you do a thorough job of completing the activities in chapter 2, providing proof supporting the skills you discuss in an interview should be fairly easy.

Key Points: Chapter 1

- No matter what type of interview you face, you must stay focused on conveying the job skills you have in order to be successful.

- There are several things you should do to have a successful interview: make a good impression, answer tough questions well, and follow up after the interview.

- By using the Three-Step Process, you can handle any interview question. First make sure you understand what is really being asked; then briefly respond to the question in a nondamaging way; and finally present your related job skills to answer the true question.

- To support the skills you discuss in interviews, you can use the Prove It technique. To use the Prove It Technique, give examples for, quantify, and list results for each job skill you present. You also must be able to relate your job skills to the position you are applying for.

Chapter 2

Knowing Yourself and What You Can Do

K nowing what you are good at is an essential part of doing well in a job interview. It is also important because unless you use the skills that you enjoy using and are good at, you are unlikely to be fully satisfied in your job.

Most people are not good at recognizing and listing the skills they have. We can tell you this based on many years of working with groups of job seekers. When asked, few people can quickly say what they are good at (other than being a "people person," a "diligent worker," or some other vague skill set), and fewer still can quickly and accurately present the specific skills that are needed to succeed in the job they want.

Many employers also note that most job seekers don't present their skills effectively. According to one survey of employers, more than 80 percent of the people they interview cannot adequately define the skills they have that support their ability to do the job. Many job seekers have the necessary skills, but they can't communicate that fact. This chapter is designed to help you fix that problem.

Learn the Three Types of Skills

Simple skills such as closing your fingers to grip a pen are building blocks for more complex skills, such as writing a sentence, and even more complex skills, such as writing a book. Even though you have hundreds of skills, some will be more important to an employer than others. Some will be far more important to you in deciding what sort of job you want. To simplify the task of skill identification, I have found it useful to think of skills in three major categories: self-management skills, transferable skills, and job-related skills.

Self-Management Skills

The skills in this set are often called *adaptive skills, personality traits,* or even *fitting-in skills* because they allow you to adapt or adjust to a variety of situations. These skills also have a lot to do with your job satisfaction and your ability to be happy and productive on the job. For example, a machine operator who isn't detailed, careful, quick, productive, and precise will have a hard time meeting her quota for making high-quality parts.

Many of the skills/traits in this skills set could be considered part of your basic personality. Such skills, which are highly valued by employers, include getting to work on time, honesty, enthusiasm, and getting along with others.

And if you happen to be someone with limited work experience, you're in luck. Most employers are willing to train a person who lacks some job-related skills but displays good self-management skills. Some employers even prefer job seekers with better self-management skills than job-related skills because those job seekers are more trainable and not set in former ways.

The Skills Employers Want

To illustrate that employers value self-management skills very highly, here are the results of a survey of employers. This information comes from a study of employers called *Workplace Basics: The Skills Employers Want.* The study was conducted jointly by the U.S. Department of Labor and the American Association of Counseling and Development.

It turns out that many of the skills employers want are self-management skills. Of course, specific job-related skills remain important, but basic skills form an essential foundation for success on the job. Here are the top skills employers identified:

1. Learning to learn

2. Basic academic skills in reading, writing, and computation

3. Good communication skills, including listening and speaking

4. Creative thinking and problem solving

5. Self-esteem, motivation, and goal setting

6. Personal and career development skills

7. Interpersonal/negotiation skills and teamwork

8. Organizational effectiveness and leadership

What is most interesting is that most of these skills are not formally taught in school. Yet these so-called soft skills are what employers value most. Of course, job-related skills are also important (an accountant still needs to know accounting skills), but self-management skills are the ones that enable you to succeed in any job.

Again, this study shows the importance of being aware of your skills and using them well in career planning. If you have any weaknesses in one or more of the preceding skills, consider improvements. Always remember to turn your weaknesses into strengths. For example, if you don't have a specific skill that's required for a job, let the employer know that you don't, but add that you are eager to learn and you are a quick study. This comment shows the employer that you are not afraid of learning new skills and that you are confident in your abilities. Furthermore, if you are already strong in one or more of the top skills employers want, look for opportunities to develop and use that skill or skills in your work or to present them clearly in your next interview.

Transferable Skills

Transferable skills, sometimes called *value-added skills,* are frequently overlooked by unprepared job seekers during an interview. Possessing skills from this set tells the employer that you can bring more to the table by doing more than just the job you've applied for. In other words, you bring added value to the employer.

Transferable skills are general skills that can be useful in a variety of jobs but might not be specifically required to do the job being sought. For example, a framing carpenter who can train other workers has the job-related skill of framing walls and the transferable skill of training. Writing clearly, strong language skills, or the ability to organize and prioritize tasks are desirable transferable skills for many jobs. These skills are called transferable because they can be transferred from one job—or even one career—to another. If you're changing careers, entering the workforce for the first time, leaving the military, returning to work after raising a family, or leaving prison for a new life, it's imperative that you develop the ability to identify in yourself and articulate your possession of these skills during the interview.

Job-Related Skills

Job-related skills are sometimes called *screening skills* because these are the skills that employers use to screen you into, or out of, an interview. If you don't have these, you can't do the job. These are also skills people typically think of first when asked, "Do you have any skills?" Job-related skills are directly related to a particular job or type of job. An auto mechanic, for example, needs to know how to tune engines or repair brakes. Every job has a "career vocabulary" and a list of keywords that go with the occupation. If you are a welder and you see the words 60/40 rod, mig, tig, and heliarch, you should know these are a few of the words used in a welder's career vocabulary.

Identify Your Skills

Being aware of your skills is extremely important. To help you discover more about your own skills we've included a series of checklists and other activities in this chapter to help you identify your key skills. Recognizing your skills is important for doing well in a job interview. After completing the following activities, you'll be able to articulate your skills in tomorrow's interview with ease.

Learning about your own skills can also be very helpful to you in writing resumes and conducting your job search. For more information on those topics, check out some other great titles from JIST (www.jist.com).

To begin exploring the skills you posses, answer the question in the following box.

WHAT MAKES YOU A GOOD WORKER?

On the following lines, list up to ten skills/traits matching each skill set that you think make you a good worker. You can find lists of skills in each set on pages 21, 24, and 26. Take your time. Think about what an employer might like about you or the way you work.

Self-Management	Transferable	Job-Related

Your goal should be to have at least 30 skills you can name for an employer, and you should strive to support each one with a concrete example during the interview. The skills you just wrote down might be the most important things that an employer wants to know about you.

If you had any trouble defining your skills, don't be discouraged. Eighty percent of job seekers are in the same boat, and there are more exercises following that will be a big help.

Identify Your Self-Management Skills and Personality Traits

Following is a list of the self-management skills that tend to be important to employers. The ones listed under "The Minimum" are those that most employers consider essential for job survival, and many employers will not hire someone who has problems in these areas.

Look over the list and put a check mark next to each self-management skill you possess. Pay careful attention to those skills you notice that will most likely be important for you to use or include in your next job.

SELF-MANAGEMENT SKILLS WORKSHEET

The Minimum

____ Have good attendance	____ Meet deadlines
____ Am honest	____ Get along with supervisors
____ Arrive on time	____ Get along with coworkers
____ Follow instructions	____ Am hardworking and productive

Other Self-Management Skills

____ Coordinating	____ Intuitive	____ Problem-solving
____ Results-oriented	____ Decisive	____ Team player
____ Mentoring	____ Multicultural	____ Multitasking
____ Friendly	____ Discreet	____ Patient

(continued)

(continued)

___ Ambitious	___ Quick learner	___ Spontaneous
___ Good-natured	___ Eager	___ Persistent
___ Assertive	___ Loyal	___ Steady
___ Helpful	___ Efficient	___ Physically strong
___ Capable	___ Mature	___ Tactful
___ Humble	___ Energetic	___ Practical
___ Cheerful	___ Methodical	___ Proud of work
___ Imaginative	___ Enthusiastic	___ Competent
___ Modest	___ Reliable	___ Independent
___ Expressive	___ Tenacious	___ Well-organized
___ Motivated	___ Resourceful	___ Industrious
___ Flexible	___ Thrifty	___ Natural
___ Responsible	___ Conscientious	___ Formal
___ Trustworthy	___ Informal	___ Open-minded
___ Self-confident	___ Creative	___ Optimistic
___ Versatile	___ Intelligent	___ Sincere
___ Humorous	___ Dependable	___ Original

Other Similar Self-Management Skills You Have

Add any self-management skills that were not listed but that you think are important to include:

_____   _____

_____   _____

_____   _____

_____   _____

_____   _____

Your Top Self-Management Skills

Carefully review the checklist you just completed and select the 10 self-management skills you feel are most important for you to tell an employer about or that you most want to use in your next job. The skills you choose are *extremely* important to present to an employer in an interview.

1. _____   6. _____

2. _____   7. _____

3. _____   8. _____

4. _____   9. _____

5. _____   10. _____

The information you gained from doing this exercise should help you better answer personality-based questions such as "How would you describe yourself (your personality)?" and "What makes you think you would fit in with this company?"

Identify Your Transferable Skills

In the checklist that follows, the skills listed under "The Minimum" are those that we consider to be most important for success on the job. These skills are also those most often required in jobs with more responsibility and higher pay, so emphasize these skills if you have them.

The remaining transferable skills after "The Minimum" are grouped into categories that might be helpful to you. Go ahead and check each skill you are strong in, and take note of the skills you want to use or think will be important in your next job. When you are finished, you should have checked 10 to 20 skills at least once.

TRANSFERABLE SKILLS CHECKLIST

The Minimum

____ Meet deadlines   ____ Solve problems

____ Plan   ____ Manage money or budgets

____ Speak in public   ____ Manage people

____ Control budgets   ____ Supervise others

____ Handle the public   ____ Increase sales or efficiency

____ Negotiate   ____ Accept responsibility

____ Instruct others   ____ Write

____ Organize   ____ Manage projects

____ Use technology/computers
   to perform a job

Physical

____ Drive or operate vehicles   ____ Spray, paint, roll liquids

____ Assemble or make things   ____ Carry, lift, haul items

____ Build, construct things   ____ Observe or inspect things

____ Repair or replace things   ____ Do precision work

Dealing with Data

____ Analyze data or facts   ____ Negotiate

____ Investigate   ____ Compare, inspect, record facts

____ Audit records   ____ Count, observe, compile

____ Keep financial records   ____ Research

____ Budget   ____ Pay attention to detail

____ Locate answers or information   ____ Synthesize

____ Calculate, compute   ____ Evaluate

____ Manage money   ____ Take inventory

____ Classify data   ____ Technologically analyze data

Working with People

____ Administer   ____ Be pleasant   ____ Be diplomatic

____ Show patience   ____ Counsel people   ____ Supervise

____ Care for others   ____ Be sensitive   ____ Help others

____ Persuade   ____ Demonstrate   ____ Socialize

____ Be tactful   ____ Have insight   ____ Confront others

____ Teach   ____ Be tough   ____ Understand

____ Interview others   ____ Listen   ____ Be outgoing

____ Be tolerant   ____ Trust   ____ Be kind

____ Negotiate   ____ Follow directions   ____ Demonstrate

Using Words and Ideas

____ Be articulate   ____ Correspond with others

____ Design   ____ Invent

____ Speak in public   ____ Communicate verbally

____ Remember information   ____ Edit

____ Write clearly   ____ Think logically

____ Research   ____ Be ingenious

____ Create new ideas   ____ Persuade with words

Leadership

____ Arrange social functions   ____ Direct others

____ Motivate people   ____ Exercise self-control

____ Be competitive   ____ Explain things to others

(continued)

(continued)

____ Negotiate agreements   ____ Motivate yourself

____ Make decisions   ____ Get results

____ Plan   ____ Solve problems

____ Delegate   ____ Mediate problems

____ Run meetings   ____ Take risks

Creative/Artistic

____ Be artistic   ____ Perform, act

____ Express yourself   ____ Present artistic ideas

____ Appreciate music   ____ Draw

____ Dance   ____ Play instruments

Your Top Transferable Skills

Carefully review the checklist you just completed and select the 10 transferable skills you feel are most important for you to tell an employer about or that you most want to use in your next job. The skills you choose are *extremely* important to present to an employer in an interview.

1. _____   6. _____

2. _____   7. _____

3. _____   8. _____

4. _____   9. _____

5. _____   10. _____

Identify Your Job-Related Skills

Many jobs require skills that are specific to that occupation. An airline pilot obviously needs to know how to fly an airplane. Thankfully, having good self-management and transferable skills would not be enough to be considered for that job.

Job-related skills come from a variety of sources, including education, training, work, hobbies, and life experience. As you complete the following exercises, pay special attention to those experiences and accomplishments that you really enjoyed. When discussing these skills in your interview, quantify your responses with numbers. Employers can relate more easily to percentages, raw numbers, and ratios than to quality terms such as *more*, *many*, *greater*, *less*, *fewer*, and so on. For example, saying "effectively presented product pitch to groups as large as 200 people and garnered 20 percent more sales than competitive presenters" has more impact than "did many presentations for large groups and made more sales than others."

The following exercises will help you investigate the job-related skills you possess and how you acquired them and have demonstrated them in the past. A checklist for these skills would be overwhelming because they are industry specific. However, these exercises will enable you to create your own list of job-related skills.

The following Education and Training Worksheet helps you review all your education and training experiences, even those that might have occurred years ago. Some courses might seem more important to certain careers than others. But keep in mind that even the courses that don't seem to support a particular career choice can be important sources of skills.

EDUCATION AND TRAINING WORKSHEET

Everyone gains work experience in the same three ways: through life experiences, through paid and volunteer work experiences, and through educational experiences.

Many of your educational experiences are directly applicable to the labor market. It's your job to show the employer how your educational background will transfer to your next job. A few examples of educational skills transferring to the workplace are the following:

- Working collectively on a project as a part of a team.

- Using technology to perform research activities.

- Meeting deadlines by completing homework on time.

Try to list a few examples of your educational skills that can transfer to the workplace.

(continued)

(continued)

1. _____

2. _____

3. _____

4. _____

5. _____

Learning how to link your education to an employer's needs is important during an interview. But it's even more important if you're a newly graduated student or someone who has limited work experience.

Elementary Grades

Although few employers will ask you about these years, jot down any highlights of things you felt particularly good about. Doing so might help you identify important interests and directions to consider for the future. For example, note the following:

- Subjects you did well in that might relate to the job you want

- Extracurricular activities/hobbies/leisure activities

- Accomplishments/things you did well (in or out of school)

_____

_____

_____

_____

High School Experiences

These experiences will be more important for a recent high school graduate and less important for those with college, work, or other life experiences. But whatever your situation, what you did during these years might demonstrate applicable job skills.

Name of school(s)/years attended:

_____

_____

Subjects you did well in or that might relate to the job you want:

_____

_____

_____

Extracurricular activities/hobbies/leisure activities:

_____

_____

_____

Accomplishments/things you did well (in or out of school):

_____

_____

_____

Volunteer or high school work activities:

_____

_____

_____

Postsecondary or College Experiences

If you attended or graduated from a two- or four-year college or took college classes, what you learned and did during this time will often be of interest to an employer. If you are a new graduate, these experiences can be particularly important because you have less work experience to present. Emphasize here those things that directly support your ability to do the job. For example, working your way through school shows that you are hardworking. If you took courses that specifically support your job, you can include details on those as well.

(continued)

(continued)

Name of school(s)/years attended:

_____

_____

Major: _____

Courses related to job objective:

_____

_____

_____

_____

Extracurricular activities/hobbies/leisure activities:

_____

_____

_____

_____

Accomplishments/things you did well (in or out of school):

_____

_____

_____

_____

_____

_____

Specific things you learned or can do that relate to the job you want:

_____

_____

_____

_____

Additional Training and Education

There are many formal and informal ways to learn, and some of the most important things are often learned outside of the classroom. Use this worksheet to list any additional training or education that might relate to the job you want. Include military training, on-the-job training, workshops, or any other formal or informal training you have had. You can also include any substantial learning you obtained through a hobby, family activity, online research, or similar informal source.

On-the-job training (name of courses or programs, dates course was taken, any certificates or credentials earned):

_____

_____

_____

On-line instruction (name of class and rationale for taking the class):

_____

_____

_____

Self-learned abilities (such as how to operate a computer, how to repair a motorcycle, or home maintenance):

_____

_____

_____

Any other skills you have that could relate to the job you're interviewing for:

_____

_____

_____

JOB AND VOLUNTEER HISTORY WORKSHEET

Use this worksheet to list each major job you have held. Begin with your most recent job, followed by previous ones.

Include military experience and unpaid volunteer work here, too. Both are work and are particularly important if you do not have much paid civilian work experience. If you have been promoted, consider handling the new position as a separate job from the original position.

Whenever possible, provide numbers to support what you did such as the number of transactions processed, percentage of sales increase, total budget you were responsible for, or other specific data.

Job #1

Name of organization: _____

Address:_____

Job title(s): _____

Employed from: _____ to: _____

Computers, software, or other machinery or equipment you used:

_____

_____

_____

Data, information, or reports you created or used:

_____

_____

_____

People-oriented duties or responsibilities to coworkers, customers, others:

_____

_____

_____

_____

_____

Services you provided or products you produced:

_____

_____

_____

_____

Reasons for promotions or salary increases, if any:

_____

_____

_____

_____

What success and achievements are you proud of on this job? Detail out anything you did to help the organization, such as increase productivity, improve procedures or processes, simplify or reorganize job duties, decrease costs, increase profits, improve working conditions, reduce turnover, or other improvements. Quantify results when possible; use statements such as, "Increased order processing by 50 percent, with no increase in staff costs."

_____

_____

_____

_____

What specific things did you learn or skills did you develop that relate to the job you want?

_____

_____

(continued)

(continued)

_____

_____

_____

What would your (former) coworkers say about you?

_____

_____

_____

What would your (former) supervisor say about you?

_____

_____

_____

Supervisor's name: _____

Phone number:_____ E-mail address: _____

Job #2

Name of organization: _____

Address:_____

Job title(s): _____

Employed from: _____ to: _____

Computers, software, or other machinery or equipment you used:

_____

_____

_____

Data, information, or reports you created or used:

_____

_____

_____

People-oriented duties or responsibilities to coworkers, customers, others:

_____

_____

_____

_____

_____

Services you provided or products you produced:

_____

_____

_____

_____

_____

Reasons for promotions or salary increases, if any:

_____

_____

_____

_____

_____

What success and achievements are you proud of on this job? Detail out anything you did to help the organization, such as increase productivity, improve procedures or processes, simplify or reorganize job duties, decrease costs, increase profits, improve working conditions, reduce turnover, or other improvements. Quantify results when possible; use statements such as, "Increased order processing by 50 percent with no increase in staff costs."

_____

_____

(continued)

(continued)

_____

_____

What specific things did you learn or skills did you develop that relate to the job you want?

_____

_____

_____

_____

What would your (former) coworkers say about you?

_____

_____

_____

What would your (former) supervisor say about you?

_____

_____

_____

Supervisor's name: _____

Phone number: _____ E-mail address: _____

Job #3

Name of organization: _____

Address: _____

Job title(s): _____

Employed from: _____ to: _____

Computers, software, or other machinery or equipment you used:

_____

_____

_____

Data, information, or reports you created or used:

_____

_____

_____

People-oriented duties or responsibilities to coworkers, customers, others:

_____

_____

_____

_____

_____

Services you provided or products you produced:

_____

_____

_____

_____

_____

Reasons for promotions or salary increases, if any:

_____

_____

_____

_____

_____

(continued)

(continued)

What success and achievements are you proud of on this job? Detail out anything you did to help the organization, such as increase productivity, improve procedures or processes, simplify or reorganize job duties, decrease costs, increase profits, improve working conditions, reduce turnover, or other improvements. Quantify results when possible; use statements such as, "Increased order processing by 50 percent with no increase in staff costs."

_____

_____

_____

_____

What specific things did you learn or skills did you develop that relate to the job you want?

_____

_____

_____

_____

What would your (former) coworkers say about you?

_____

_____

_____

What would your (former) supervisor say about you?

_____

_____

_____

Supervisor's name: _____

Phone number:_____ E-mail address: _____

Job #4

Name of organization: _____

Address:_____

Job title(s): _____

Employed from: _____ to: _____

Computers, software, or other machinery or equipment you used:

_____

_____

_____

Data, information, or reports you created or used:

_____

_____

_____

People-oriented duties or responsibilities to coworkers, customers, others:

_____

_____

_____

_____

_____

Services you provided or products you produced:

_____

_____

_____

_____

_____

(continued)

(continued)

Reasons for promotions or salary increases, if any:

_____

_____

_____

_____

_____

What success and achievements are you proud of on this job? Detail out anything you did to help the organization, such as increase productivity, improve procedures or processes, simplify or reorganize job duties, decrease costs, increase profits, improve working conditions, reduce turnover, or other improvements. Quantify results when possible; use statements such as, "Increased order processing by 50 percent with no increase in staff costs."

_____

_____

_____

_____

What specific things did you learn or skills did you develop that relate to the job you want?

_____

_____

_____

What would your (former) coworkers say about you?

_____

_____

_____

What would your (former) supervisor say about you?

_____

_____

_____

Supervisor's name: _____

Phone number:_____ E-mail address: _____

OTHER LIFE EXPERIENCES WORKSHEET

People often overlook informal life experiences as sources of learning or accomplishment. Think about any hobbies or interests you have had: family responsibilities, recreational activities, travel, or any other experiences in your life that have given you some sense of accomplishment. List any experiences that seem particularly meaningful to you and name the key skills you think were involved.

Situation 1:

Describe the situation and skills used:

_____

_____

_____

_____

Specific things you learned or can do that relate to the job you want:

_____

_____

_____

_____

(continued)

(continued)

Situation 2:

Describe the situation and skills used:

_____

_____

_____

_____

Specific things you learned or can do that relate to the job you want:

_____

_____

_____

_____

Situation 3:

Describe the situation and skills used:

_____

_____

_____

_____

Specific things you learned or can do that relate to the job you want:

_____

_____

_____

_____

YOUR TOP JOB-RELATED SKILLS

Carefully review the exercises you just completed and select the 10 job-related skills you feel are most important for you to tell an employer about or that you most want to use in your next job. The skills you choose are *extremely* important to present to an employer in an interview.

1. _____   6. _____

2. _____   7. _____

3. _____   8. _____

4. _____   9. _____

5. _____   10. _____

Key Points: Chapter 2

- Knowing your skills is essential for answering most interview questions. Once you develop your "skills language," you can use it to help identify how you would be useful to an employer, present your work history in its best light, and set yourself apart from other merely technically qualified applicants.

- Self-management skills such as having good work habits and working well with others are important to employers.

- Transferable skills, which include writing, managing people, and analyzing data, are useful in many different careers. Be sure to emphasize your relevant transferable skills in interviews.

- Job-related skills are those skills you have learned through education, training, and job experience. When you discuss these skills in an interview, provide as many numbers, examples, and results as you can.

Chapter 3

Researching the Industry, Company, Job, and Interviewer

E mployers point out that one of the most common mistakes job seekers make is coming to the interview without some knowledge of the company to which they are applying. "Know thyself" used to be the key phrase in career development. A good many people walk into the interview well prepared to speak about themselves and their accomplishments, but they lack adequate knowledge about the industry or field, the company and its culture, the demands of the job, and the interviewer. If knowledge is a driving force in interview success, job seekers without information on these four things will be at a serious disadvantage during the interview.

A well-prepared interviewee has done research on at least these four things:

- Industry
- Company and its culture
- Job task
- Interviewer

Unfortunately, gaining knowledge on these requires research, and many people resist doing it. Their lack of preparation often shows in the interview. This chapter takes the mystery out of research by pointing out where to turn, what to look for, and how to have fun doing it.

Industry Research

This type of research information is often called field and trend research. The industry information you gather will be invaluable to you during the interview process. Let's say that you have an interview tomorrow in a hospital. Even if you hope to work in a nonmedical area such as accounting, you will do better in the interview if you know something about the health care industry.

Employers want people who are problem solvers and future focused. By researching the industry, the field, and its trends, you can walk into the interview and demonstrate your ability to identify common problems faced in your industry and also point to future trends in your industry that you've discovered. A few types of information you should acquire include the following:

- The latest trends in your chosen career field

- Any environmental or political factors affecting the industry

- New technologies, equipment, or methods coming soon

- Common problems within this industry or field

- The number of companies in the industry

- Professional organizations supporting the industry

- Trade and professional journals of the industry

- Projected employment growth of the industry

- Pay and compensation packages within the industry

- Training or education that will be needed

The following resources can help you find information on any industry in which you might be interested in working.

Written Publications to Help You Find Out About Industries

Out of the hundreds of sources of career information, an important few will give you most of what you need. We've listed these few primary resources here, along with information on where to find them.

Career Guide to Industries

This book, published by the U.S. Department of Labor, is of particular value to job seekers. It provides helpful descriptions for 44 major industries, which cover about 75 percent of all jobs. The *Career Guide to Industries* is easy to read and provides information that can help you present yourself well in an interview.

Each description includes an overview of the nature of the industry, working conditions, employment projections, types of jobs it offers, training and advancement, earnings, sources of additional information, and more. You can find the *Career Guide to Industries* in your local library or bookstore. You can also access its contents online at http://stats.bls.gov/oco/cg/home.htm.

The *Occupational Outlook Handbook*

We consider the *Occupational Outlook Handbook (OOH)* to be one of the most helpful books on career information available. If you have time, buy one (visit your local bookstore or www.jist.com) because it is useful in a variety of ways. You can also access the *OOH* information online at www.bls.gov/oco.

The *OOH* provides descriptions for about 270 of America's most popular jobs, organized within clusters of related jobs. Although that number may not sound like many jobs, about 87 percent of the workforce works in these jobs.

The *OOH* is updated every two years by the U.S. Department of Labor and provides the latest information on salaries, growth projections, related jobs, required skills, education or training needed, working conditions, and many other details. Each job is described in a readable, interesting format.

You can use the *OOH* in many ways. Here are some suggestions:

- **Identify the skills needed for the job you want.** Look up a job that interests you, and the *OOH* tells you the transferable and job-related skills it requires. Assuming that you have these skills, you can then emphasize them in interviews.

- **Find skills from previous jobs that support your present objective.** Look up *OOH* descriptions for jobs you have had in the past. A careful read will help you identify skills that can be transferred and used in the new job. Even "minor" jobs can be valuable in this way. For example, if you waited tables while going to school, you would discover that this job requires the ability to work under pressure, deal with customers, and work quickly. Or, if you are now looking for a job as an accountant, you can cross-reference the transferable skills you used as a salesman with the skills required to be an accountant. If you are changing careers or don't have much work experience related to the job you want, describing your transferable skills can be very important.

- **Find out the typical salary range, trends, and other details.** The *OOH* helps you know what pay range to expect and which trends affect the job. Note that local pay averages and other details can differ significantly from the national information provided in the *OOH*.

- **Find more sources for information on your target job.** Each *OOH* job description provides helpful sources, including a cross-reference to the O*NET career information (see the next section), related professional associations, Internet sites, and other sources.

Trade Publications and Magazines

A good library offers lots of information on industries. Industry trade magazines such as *Advertising Age, Automotive News, Hotel & Motel Management, Modern Healthcare,* and *Supermarket News* are full of articles detailing trends and problems in particular industries. Grab the last six months of issues and skim through if time is getting tight or settle down for some interesting reading.

While you have these publications in hand at the library, photocopy and highlight facts that support your position in that industry, and scribble in the margins some questions you'd like your prospective employer to answer. And always flip to the classifieds section—no use wasting a perfectly good chance to find another job lead!

Find Magazines Online

Many trade magazines also maintain Web sites. Here are a few sites to get you started:

- **Yahoo!:** http://dir.yahoo.com/Business_and_Economy/ Business_to_Business/News_and_Media/Magazines/ Trade_Magazines/

- **Your Trade Pubs:** www.yourtradepubs.com

- **Free Trade Magazine Source:** www.freetrademagazinesource.com

- **Business Magazine Network:** http://the.businessmagazinenetwork.com

- **Mag Portal:** www.magportal.com

Encyclopedia of Associations

Every industry has an association to which it belongs. Grab the library's current copy of the *Encyclopedia of Associations.* Don't let its name intimidate you; it's a gold mine of associations listed by categories. Each entry gives the contact information, mission statement, newsletters, and conventions for that group. Pick the ones in your industry category that closely match your situation and give them a call or check out their Web sites. They will most likely provide useful information on recent happenings in your industry, and you can request copies of a recent newsletter or journal to study before future interviews.

Industry Research on the Internet

There are literally hundreds—maybe thousands— of Web sites for researching industries, but you need to prepare today for an interview tomorrow…and you don't have much time to dedicate to doing research. So here are a few good Web sites that will provide you with the necessary information about your target industry.

Hoover's Online

This site is operated by a Dunn and Bradstreet company. You can visit it to find anything you need to know about your industry and future employer. Basic information is free. More detailed information will cost you. You can search for information by company name, industry type, stock ticker, and so on.

www.hoovers.com

Wetfeet

As a starting point to gathering industry information, try Wetfeet. It's one of the best compilations of research information online and provides other job search and research links.

www.wetfeet.com

Polson Enterprises: Researching an Industry or Specific Company

This site provides you with an organized way to research an industry as well as specific companies. It features a number of relevant links that you'll find useful in your research activities.

www.virtualpet.com/industry/howto/search.htm

Yahoo! Industry News

This site will help you check industry press releases and current news on a wide array of industries.

http://biz.yahoo.com/industry/

IndustryLink

This site describes itself as the premier directory of links to industry Web sites.

www.industrylink.com

Google News

Search and browse 4,500 news sources to find the most up-to-date news stories on specific companies and fields. Articles stay in the index for 30 days.

http://news.google.com

Company and Cultural Research

The best sources for information on *local* organizations are local newspaper articles, local directories, and area trade journals. Some libraries keep clipping files of articles on area companies, CEOs, and industries. Ask a reference librarian for ranked lists of local companies in your field. Depending on the library's size, you might even lay your hands on annual reports and various promotional literature, too.

Getting Company Information from the Company

If you want to receive literature and materials from your target organization itself, offer to drop by and pick them up in person. You can do this today if your interview is tomorrow. This action also fosters several positives. It allows you to meet with the receptionist and make a positive impression with an insider (good news travels fast, especially when it concerns a future employee). It also strengthens an impression that you are well-organized and very interested. Finally, it forces you to travel the route in advance of an interview and scout out potentially slowing traffic patterns, confusing addresses, and so on.

(continued)

(continued)

> If there's time, see if it's possible to get a tour of the facility. It's impressive to say that you took a tour that strengthened your desire to work for the company.

If the organization is a small, privately owned company, literature on it might not be available at all. In that case, research comparable companies and apply what you find. Don't forget—it's never a mistake to pick up the phone and talk with the organization's suppliers, customers, and current employees.

Granted, translating columns of numbers and sales slogans into tangible answers to the questions you'll be asked takes some thoughtful application on your part. However, don't let it scare you into not trying. Be sure to read the CEO's message at the beginning of the company's annual report. This carefully crafted editorial sets the tone for the past year and the organization's direction in the years ahead.

> **Tip:** *Stop by your local One-Stop Career Center (www.servicelocator.org) or your school's career center if you're a student or graduate, and see whether they have any information that will give you some insight into your target company and its culture.*

Company Research

After researching the industry, you can get more specific and research your target company. Obviously, information about the company is critical for answering the interview question, "What do you know about the company?"

Essential Questions Your Research Must Answer

The following are some more basic questions you want to find answers to when doing company research:

- What does the company make, do, or sell?
- How has the company been doing (downsizing history, sales history, hiring history, and so on)?

- How did the company start up and who were the people responsible for starting it?

- Who are the company's biggest competitors?

- What new products or services is the company going to offer in the near future?

- How large is the company (number of employees, gross sales figures, and so on) and are there other company locations?

- How has the company set itself apart from its competition?

- How would you describe the culture in the company (for example, family friendly, employee friendly, production oriented, and so on)?

- Will the job you are pursuing contribute to the organization's success?

Online Company Research Sites

One of the easiest ways to gather company information is to start with simple Internet searches. Here are a few of the Web sites that will do you the most good in the shortest amount of time.

- The company's Web site

- Better Business Bureau: www.bbb.org

- Monster Company Boulevard:http://company.monster.com

- Vault: www.vault.com

- Quintessential Careers Directory of Company Career Centers: www.quintcareers.com/career_centers/

- Thomas Register: www.thomasnet.com

- Corporate Information: www.corporateinformation.com

Company Research Tutorials

For tips and instructions on researching employers, check out these Web sites:

- **Industry Research Desk (www.virtualpet.com/industry/):** This 19-step process walks you through researching a specific company or industry. A ton of links to useful resources are

(continued)

(continued)

included among the steps, so take some time to explore. You'll also find ideas on potentially useful print resources that you can look through at your local library.

- **Researching Companies Online (www.learnwebskills.com/company/):** This step-by-step tutorial from Internet trainer Debbie Flanagan contains surefire tips for locating free company and industry information on the Web. Topics here include locating company home pages, monitoring company news, learning about an industry, identifying international business resources, and researching nonprofit organizations. Each topic includes useful links and instructions, and you can also access her Web Search Strategies tutorial from here.

- **Riley Guide: Using the Internet to Do Job Search Research (www.rileyguide.com/jsresearch.html):** The first section provides general tips on doing effective Internet research. The second gives specific advice on finding company information. This step-by-step tutorial shows you how to do research on all aspects of your job search. It links to a number of sites for additional information and ideas.

Job Task Analysis Research

Beyond researching the company and industry, you also need to research the job you will be expected to perform. This research helps you define the demands of the job for which you're applying and enables you to answer interview questions such as the following:

- Can you describe a typical workday?

- Can you give me examples of when you've done similar work?

- What do you think will be needed for success on this job?

- How long will it take you to become productive?

What to Ask

Some of the questions you should ask in doing job task analysis research include the following:

- What types of data or information will I have to use or generate on the job?

- What types of tools, machines, and equipment will I have to operate?

- What types of interpersonal interactions will I have on the job and with whom will I have to interact the most?

- Are there any production or quality quotas to meet?

- What factors make a person successful in this job?

- What are the likely physical working conditions?

- What are the keywords, buzzwords, and vernacular of the job?

- What are the most difficult parts of the job?

- What type of pay and compensation package are normal for this position?

Where to Look

Three places you can gather this type of information are the Department of Labor's O*NET, company job descriptions, peer research, and interviewer research. The following sections give more details on using each of these sources.

Department of Labor's O*NET

The U.S. Department of Labor maintains an up-to-date computer database of occupational information. Called the O*NET Occupational Information Network, it provides detailed information for almost 12,000 jobs. Although the *Occupational Outlook Handbook (OOH)* mentioned earlier is more useful for most situations, the O*NET describes many more jobs (and more specialized jobs) and provides more details on each one.

The O*NET database offers basic descriptions for each of its jobs, plus hundreds of additional data elements for each job. The O*NET database is available to view on the Internet at http://online.onetcenter.org. Keep in mind that the O*NET is a complex database and much of the detailed information it provides is not of much use for quick and focused research. Fortunately, career counselors have developed more helpful versions of the O*NET database. A book version published by JIST and titled *O*NET Dictionary of Occupational Titles* was designed to provide the O*NET information of greatest value to most job seekers in an easy-to-use book format.

Job Descriptions

Before going to any interviews, try to get your hands on a job description from the company to which you are applying. You also want to go online and do a Google search for the words "job description" along with the name of whatever type of job you've applied to. Your query results should look something like figure 3.1.

Figure 3.1: The results of searching Google for "job description" and "youth coordinator."

Try to get six or more versions of the job description and highlight the keywords, skills, buzzwords, and qualifications that you find. These are the words you want to use during the interview. Reviewing your compiled list of job description keywords, try to think of times when you've successfully performed each task or used each skill mentioned. This approach builds interview confidence quicker than any other way we've seen and will allow you to make a very positive impact on the interviewer.

Peer Research

First-hand information is better than any other type of information. If you know someone in the company, use him or her as a referral to speak with an employee doing the job you want (as long as you're not replacing that employee) or someone in a similar or complementary position. Let the person you speak with know that you're trying to research the job and offer to buy lunch, a drink, or dinner so that you can ask him or her to answer the job task analysis questions listed earlier. You can also gain some knowledge of what to expect during the interview by asking your peer the following questions:

- What questions were you asked when you were interviewed?
- What type of interview did you go through (panel, stress, behavioral, and so on)?
- What are two of the biggest problems you face on the job?
- What are some of the boss's pet peeves?
- How would you describe an "ideal candidate" for the job?

Having this type of information will really help you shine during the interview process.

Interviewer Research

The more you know about the interviewer's style, methods, pet peeves, and what they're looking for from the ideal candidate, the easier it is to convince him or her that you're the right person for the job. Any kind of good connection you can make with the interviewer will be beneficial. Being members of the same clubs or church, former schoolmates, or parents of kids going to the same school helps. Even just knowing something personal about the interviewer's background can put a couple of extra interview points on the scoreboard for you. There are a few simple ways to do this type of research:

- Ask people you know at the company about the interviewer.
- Google the interviewer's name in quotation marks. Because there are many people with the same names, you'll need to sort through the results to find relevant information about the right person.
- Hit the company's Web site to see whether there's a profile of the person or persons interviewing you.

- Call the secretary and see whether he or she can give you any insight into the interviewer.

- See if the interviewer holds a membership in the Society for Human Resource Management (www.shrm.org). If so, there's probably a profile for him or her.

A few things you should try to find out about the interviewer include the following:

- What professional organizations or associations does he or she belong to, and is he or she an elected officer?

- How has this person distinguished him- or herself (honors, awards, publications, and so on)?

- How is he or she perceived within the company?

- Is this the person who makes the final hiring decision?

- Does this person have the power to negotiate pay and benefits?

- Does the interviewer belong to any social groups, such as the Lions Club, Masons, Elks, and so on?

- Where did the interviewer go to school?

- Was the interviewer involved in any extracurricular activities in school, such as sports, fraternities/sororities, academic clubs, and so on?

- What style of interview can you expect and what types of questions does this interviewer normally ask?

- Are there any special gripes or complaints the interviewer has with applicants?

- Has he or she done any charitable work?

With this type of information, you can walk into the interview with much higher levels of confidence, lower levels of interview stress, and reduced fear. You'll make fewer interview mistakes than your competitors who didn't invest the time or energy in doing the research.

Key Points: Chapter 3

- Being well-informed about the industry you are interviewing in will help you present yourself well in the interview and during salary negotiations.

- Learning more about your career area can help you better aim your interview responses to the skills your target job requires.

- You can find information about the employer and the position you are applying for from former or current employees, trade publications, or the company's Web site or publications. This information is indispensable in preparing for an interview.

Chapter 4

Answering Key Interview Questions

Ninety percent of people who suffer from extended unemployment (remaining out of work for longer than 26 weeks) do so because of poor interviewing skills. The implication of this is simple. Improving your performance in the interview even slightly can result in your getting a job offer over someone else. Many employers say that they would have hired someone if that person had just done a bit better in the interview. Spending a little time to learn how to answer the questions covered in this chapter can make an enormous difference to you in getting a job over other qualified applicants.

A Baker's Dozen of the Most Frequently Asked Interview Questions—and How to Answer Them

Because there are literally hundreds of interview questions you could be asked, the question becomes "Where should you focus your interview preparation energy so that it has the most impact?" It just makes sense to start preparing for the interview by developing answers to 13 of the most common "killer questions":

1. Could you tell me a little about yourself?

2. Why do you want to work here?

3. What do you know about the company?

4. Why are you leaving (or why did you leave) your last job?

5. What is your biggest weakness?

6. What are your major strengths?

7. Why should I hire you?

8. What are your plans for the future?

9. What are your pay expectations?

10. What will your former employers or coworkers say about you?

11. How does your previous experience relate to this job?

12. Why did you select this line of work, career path, or field?

13. Could you tell me about your personal situation?

In this chapter, the focus is on answering these 13 questions. The following chapter targets answering interview questions about sensitive topics or situations such as age, disabilities, felonies, overqualification, and so on.

Question #1: "Could You Tell Me a Little About Yourself?"

This question is usually asked early in the interview. You should have a one- to two-minute presentation that highlights your value; expresses your interest in the company and the field; and summarizes your skills, abilities, and successful experiences. This one- to two-minute performance will either set the stage for a positive and enjoyable interviewing experience, or it will make the rest of the interview a nightmare!

Skip the Chit-Chat

One big mistake you might be tempted to make is to begin talking about the wrong things such as how many kids you have, your disabilities or weaknesses, what you can't do versus what you can do, what your spouse does for a living, your age, your social interests, your medical conditions, and so on. Although some books might encourage you to start with chit-chat by looking for something in the interviewer's office and commenting on it as a way of ingratiating yourself, there's no data to support this idea; and don't you think the interviewer has figured out what you're trying to do? You and the interviewer are in that room for only one reason: to find out whether you can bring more to the company than the competition. So get to it!

Answering this question correctly is so critical to interview success that we give you four different approaches as examples from which you can build your own answer.

Sample Answer #1: Skills-Based Answer

We broke down this answer so that you can see the steps needed to develop it.

1. State your name (what you want to be called); this puts the interviewer at ease if you have a difficult name to pronounce.

   As you can see, the name on my resume is William Saramoato, but I go by Bill…and don't worry about mispronouncing my last name.

2. Next, define your job and career objective, and tell the interviewer how much experience you have and where you got the experience.

   I'm really interested in your warehouse operations manager position. Being a warehouse manager is a career goal for me. I have more than six years of experience in warehouse work. I was a materials handler at Westside Warehousing for a little over a year. I spent two years in an inventory control position at Conaco Emporium, where I had to keep track of more than $4 million worth of every type of drugstore product you could imagine, including controlled substances. I had a team of five inventory clerks there that I supervised.

   I've spent the last three years as the night-shift supervisor for Morenci Shipping, where I oversee a crew of 18 material handlers. We have to load between 18 and 25 trucks on my shift every night.

3. Then give a brief summary of your most dominant job-related skills that will be required in the position (get these from the job description).

   I've had to oversee the safe receipt, storage, retrieval, and timely dispatch of millions of dollars worth of goods. I've had to meet workplace health and safety regulations, and I have been responsible for the security of the building and loss prevention. I've planned and organized the location of goods within the warehouse and dealt with lots of special requirements for stock such as chilled goods and fragile products. I've also had to learn to use three different types of computerized storage and retrieval systems. My experience ranges from the bottom to the top. I've picked, packed, and loaded trucks by hand and with a forklift. I've also managed teams of workers and dealt with personnel issues such as recruitment, training, and employee discipline.

Make sure you have in mind three examples of when you've performed each of the tasks you're presenting, in case you are asked for more detail.

4. Next you can let the interviewer know a little bit about your education, show that you're involved in continuing education (if you are), and state your GPA if it's good. If not, keep quiet.

   I worked all through high school, and I'm currently taking online leadership courses and want to end up with a degree in business management. So far I've been managing a B+ in the coursework even though I'm working a 40-hour week.

5. Then hit the interviewer with a couple of points of pride, achievements, or successes.

   I have to say there are a couple of things I'm proud of. One is my safety record. Under my supervision, we've had no lost days due to injury in over a year. My other point of pride is loss prevention. We have the lowest loss rate since the company began.

6. Next, try to slip in something that makes you a little unique.

   I don't know what the other applicants are bringing to the table, but I think one thing that makes me unique is my military background. I've had lots of military leadership training and have had to use that training in some tough work situations.

7. Let the interviewer know that you're interested in a career with this company and not just a job.

   I'm really looking for someplace where I can develop a long-term career, and I want to work with a company where I have an opportunity to learn new things and move up.

8. After all this, give the question back to the interviewer.

   Are these the types of skills, experiences, and traits you're looking for? Or what else would you like to know? Could you tell me more about the job?

When preparing a skills-based answer, use this eight-point outline as a guide. You might want to add or delete one of the points to keep your answer brief, but retain the concept of presenting a summary, generating a positive jumping-off point, and targeting something that makes you unique.

Spend some time practicing your answer so that it sounds natural, off the cuff, and not like a canned response. That is the hardest part of preparing for this question.

Sample Answer #2: Personal-History Answer

I grew up in the Southwest and have one brother and one sister. My parents both worked, and I was active in sports growing up. I always did well in school. By the time I graduated from high school, I had taken a year's worth of business courses. I knew then that I wanted to work in a business setting and had several part-time office jobs while still in high school.

After high school, I worked in a variety of business settings and learned a great deal about how various businesses run. For example, I was given complete responsibility for the daily operations of a wholesale distribution company that grossed more than $2 million a year. That was only three years after graduating from high school. In that position, I learned to supervise other people and solve problems under pressure. I also became more interested in the financial end of running a business and decided, after three years and three promotions, to seek a position where I could have more involvement in key strategies and long-term management decisions.

Notice how this applicant provided a few bits of positive personal history and then quickly turned the interviewer's attention to skills and experiences that directly related to the job.

Sample Answer #3: Defined-Focus Answer

You could ask interviewers to help you focus on the information they really want to know with a response such as this:

There's so much to tell! Would you like me to emphasize my personal history, the special training and education I have that prepared me for this sort of position, or the skills and job-related experiences I have to support my objective?

If you do this well, most employers will tell you what sorts of things they are most interested in, and you can then concentrate on giving them what they want.

Don't Be Too Honest

Honesty is always the best policy, but that adage doesn't rule out marketing yourself in the best light during an interview. Virtually all career counselors encourage you to be positive about yourself and not to consider this positive spin as unethical in any way. But those counselors will also caution you to avoid taking credit for something you don't deserve, claiming to have experience you don't have, or hyperbolizing your past performance. You can talk up your achievements, awards, and promotions without misrepresenting yourself. A job interview is also not the place to talk about an unhappy childhood or make negative comments about past employers. Instead, focus on the positive by saying that your childhood helped you become self-motivated, resilient, and a hard worker.

Sample Answer #4: An Alternative–Returning the Question

Although a skills-based answer is the best way to get the ball rolling in your favor at the start of the interview, a trick that some interviewees use to find out exactly what the interviewer is looking for is a technique called "returning the question." With this approach, you simply skip the first seven points of a skills-based answer and start by returning the question to the interviewer. It goes like this.

Interviewer: Could you tell me a little about yourself?

Applicant: I don't want to waste your time by talking about issues not important to you or relevant to the job. Can you tell me what you're looking for from your ideal candidate?

The trick here is that an interviewer tells you what he or she wants, and you tell them you have it. There are, however, two possible problems with this approach:

1. You have to be able to think on your feet. This is difficult for most people in the pressure-cooker situation of an interview.

2. The interviewer might refuse to go for this technique. Now you're back to having a weak answer.

Regardless of the approach you use in answering this question, practice is the only solution for reducing interview anxiety and setting yourself apart from the other applicants.

Question #2: "Why Do You Want to Work Here?"

If you respond with this type of answer, "I sent out 300 resumes, and you are the only company who called me for an interview," you might be in need of a brain transplant.

It is acceptable to say that you are in the market for a new job and saw a job posting, or that you are responding to a want ad; but that's not enough. The employer wants more from you.

> **Tip:** *The information you gather for answering this question could also be used in answering related questions such as "what are your future career plans?" or "what do you know about the company?"*

Research is your friend with this question. Employers like people who have researched the company and who have identified how their skills, abilities, and experiences could transfer to the new company. You also need to understand that turnover is a costly issue with employers, and every interviewer is looking for indicators of commitment from prospective employees.

So, no matter how you put together your answer, the *main theme* of your answer should be that you've done *research,* you're looking for someplace to develop a *long-term relationship,* and you want to *grow your skills.*

Sample Answer #1

> *Although I am actively searching in the job market, I'm not willing to work just anywhere. I've put in a lot of time identifying the top 10 advertising companies in this area that I'd like to work for. I talked to a couple of people who work here, and they gave me some insight into the types of people you hire. They also said you like to challenge people and give them a lot of responsibility. I want to be challenged and given a high level of responsibility in my next job. I also know that you're a growing company and you use cutting-edge graphics software and equipment. I love the look of your promotional pieces. Because I'm interested in a career, not just a job, I thought it would be worth our effort to see whether my Web-design and computer-graphics skills meet this growing company's needs.*

You can see with this answer that you don't give away everything you found out about the company—just a couple of things. This way, you can save the rest of the information you gathered to answer the question "What do you know about the company?"

Give the interviewer enough information to show that you have invested some time in making a decision about where you want to work, that you possess a couple of key skills required for the position, and that you are excited about the company.

Sample Answer #2

I made a list of all the manufacturing companies that can use my skills located within an hour of my home. Then I narrowed down that list by doing a little research about the companies and how each values its employees. This company ended up on my top-10 list of places where I might like to develop a career.

This answer uses a more specific selection factor—distance—which is a perfectly acceptable reason for selecting one company over another. And the applicant still expresses enthusiasm for the company while indicating that he or she is looking for a long-term relationship.

Question #3: "What Do You Know About the Company?"

The key to answering correctly here is the same as with the preceding question: *research*! In the past, the mantra for job seekers was "know yourself." In today's labor market, the new mantra is "know the company." The more you know about the company, its culture, and its problems, the easier it is to show your interviewer how your background can fill an employment niche within that company.

At the very least, you should generate answers to the following questions as a way to improve your answer.

- What does the company make, do, or sell?
- How has the company been doing (downsizing history, sales history, hiring history, and so on)?
- How did the company start up and who were the people responsible for starting it?
- Who are the company's biggest competitors?
- How has the company set itself apart from its competition?
- What are the company's growth strategies and long-range plans?

See "Essential Questions Your Research Must Answer" in chapter 3 for more company-information questions that you could research if you have more time.

Here's how you can turn the information you gather into a solid interview answer.

> *When I realized that I had a chance to work here, I became very excited. I'm astounded that this company, which was started in a garage, is now among the top 25 percent in the field of making extruded plastic products. And the fact that you haven't laid anyone off in the past five years while planning on expanding your product line really speaks to the future stability of this company. I think it's amazing that you will be opening an office in China and expanding further into foreign markets. This company just seems to be on its way through the roof.*
>
> *I was also pleasantly surprised to find out from the Chamber of Commerce and the Better Business Bureau that this company has never received a complaint, and even your competitors speak well of you. The workers I know here tell me you value your employees and demand that they upgrade their skills. This is exactly the type of company I've been looking for. Is my information correct? Or would you like to hear more?*

All that's been done with this answer is to take the research information and thread it through the answer—not too complex, if you've done the research.

Question #4: "Why Are You Leaving (Or Why Did You Leave) Your Last Job?"

One thing you should pay attention to with regard to this question is that employers think there are only two reasons a person leaves a job: a good reason or a bad reason. It doesn't matter whether you were fired, lost a job to downsizing, or became unemployed for some other reason; those situations will be presented later. There are seven keys to answering this question.

1. Keep your answer simple, concise, and brief.

2. *Never* badmouth a former employer, supervisor, or coworker.

3. Do not whine about having been overworked.

4. Stay positive and future-focused—regardless of your reason for leaving.

5. Remember that your interviewer has probably changed employers in the past, too.

6. Be honest.

7. Use common and acceptable reasons for changing jobs.

Some of the more common reasons people quit jobs include

- Seeking new challenges
- No upward mobility potential
- Better career opportunities
- Less commute time
- Family demands have changed
- Benefits package needs
- Relocation for whatever reason
- Want more responsibility
- Want more excitement
- Hit the top of the pay range
- Project was completed
- Wanted more desirable work schedule
- Employer is cutting back hours
- Looking to upgrade skills
- Prior company hinting at layoffs
- Changes in management
- Making a career change
- Completed educational program

Sample Answer #1

Leaving my former employer was a tough decision because I learned a lot there and I was treated well. But I just couldn't go any further with them in terms of career growth. It was a small company with limited upward mobility opportunities.

Sample Answer #2

I really wasn't looking to leave my former employer until I was told about this position. In addition to this location being closer to my home, I've wanted to spend more time using the types of equipment and machinery you have here and working in such a team-oriented environment.

Sample Answer #3

I found myself wanting more of a challenge on the job. I redesigned my position with my old employer and created more responsibility for myself, but because of the company structure, I don't have more room to grow there.

Notice that the answers are brief and specific, and say nothing bad about the former employer.

Question #5: "What Is Your Biggest Weakness?"

This question is one that frequently causes job seekers to cringe, sweat, feel tongue-tied, and look for a way out of the interview. Although a lot of people think this is a trick question, it's really not. It's called a negative balance question and is designed to put a little pressure on the applicant. By throwing you off guard, the employer can see how you might react in other high-pressure situations on the job.

> **Caution:** If money is your primary reason for leaving, an interviewer might think you'll jump ship again as soon as you hear you might be able to increase your income at another company. So, if you do present money as a reason for leaving, add a couple of other nonmonetary reasons (such as career growth and skills expansion) to shield yourself from being thought of as a mercenary and job-hopper with no company loyalty.

Although there are many different ways for people to answer this question, it usually elicits one of three types of incorrect responses. The first response goes like this:

I really don't have any major weaknesses.

That response is untrue and evasive. Another type of incorrect response is an honest one like this:

Well, I am really disorganized. I suppose I should do better at that, but my life has just been too hectic, what with the bankruptcy and embezzlement charges and all.

Although this type of response might get an *A* for honesty, it gets an *F* for interview technique.

The third common bad response is one taught in many job search classes and in lots of job search books. It's called "rolling the interviewer."

I'm a workaholic!

This approach has the job seeker trying to pull the wool over the employers' eyes. Initially this answer might sound good, but the interviewer knows what you're up to! And you still come off sounding evasive.

What's needed here is an honest but undamaging response, followed by a brief, positive presentation to counter the negative. The best approach is to present a weakness in a way that does not harm—and could help—your ability to do a good job.

Sample Answer #1

I need to learn to be more patient. I often do things myself just because I know I can do them faster and better than someone else. This trait has not let me be as good at delegating tasks as I want to be. But I am working on it. I'm now spending more time showing others how to do the things I want done and that has helped. They often do better than I expect because I am clear about explaining what I want and how I want it done.

This response could be expanded with the Prove-It technique (see chapter 1), but as is it successfully uses the Three-Step Process in answering a problem question, as described in chapter 1. Clearly the applicant understands what is really being asked and doesn't evade the question, he or she answers the question briefly in a nondamaging way, and he or she presents related skills (being a hard worker who gets things done and has experience in delegating tasks).

Sample Answer #2

There are some areas I've been working on improving. One of those areas is organizational skills. I found that I was wasting time by having to look for information that I needed on the job. My desk was a mess. I went out and bought an office space and information organization book and the tips I got from it have helped save time and reduced my frustration. My desk no longer traps everything that goes on it.

This approach is very powerful because most employers haven't heard it. It also removes the word "weakness" from the conversation. Which sounds better to you, "weakness" or "improvement"? And this answer shows the interviewer that you can think on your feet, that you can identify areas you need to work on, and that you're willing to take the initiative to do something to correct your flaws. These are all desired characteristics that employers seek.

Question #6: "What Are Your Major Strengths?"

This is a question without any hidden meaning that allows you the chance for a little self-promoting. According to Dick Bolles, the author of *What Color Is Your Parachute?*, there are three primary employment strength areas: interpersonal strengths, mental strengths, and physical strengths.

To develop a good answer, first review your list of job-related skills, self-management skills, and transferable skills. After this, there are three exercises to further build an answer. All require self-assessment of your skills, abilities, and experiences.

Exercise #1

In the following grid, write what you consider to be your best mental, interpersonal, and physical skills.

Mental Skills	Interpersonal Skills	Physical Skills
_____	_____	_____
_____	_____	_____
_____	_____	_____
_____	_____	_____
_____	_____	_____

Exercise #2

Review your list of skills. Ask yourself which ones can be best supported with documented proof. List them below.

_____

_____

_____

_____

Exercise #3

If you're still having trouble, another way to jump-start your brain and help build a good answer is by reviewing the following list of desired employee traits.

Check up to five traits that you can claim as strengths and that you can confidently present and back up during the interview.

❑ I look for ways to work smarter.

❑ I always look for ways to save money and time.

❑ I have good listening skills and pay close attention.

❑ I enjoy working and I smile a lot—it's contagious.

❑ My production is always higher than the average.

❑ I'm loyal and dedicated to my employer.

❑ I don't expect to get ahead without doing extra work.

❑ I have a documented history of achievements and successes.

❑ I try to think things through and solve problems.

❑ I can learn new things quickly.

❑ I can work under minimal supervision.

❑ I'm an efficient worker and don't waste time.

❑ I take pride in doing quality work.

❑ I'll jump in and help others when needed.

❑ I'm willing to start at the bottom to get to the top.

❑ My attendance and punctuality are above average.

❑ I'm very safety-oriented.

❑ I'll work overtime, weekends, and holidays.

❑ I'm motivated to do good work and ask questions.

❑ I don't misuse the company's time and materials.

❑ I have a solid knowledge of this job's demands.

❑ I have good communication and interpersonal skills.

❑ I have confidence in my ability to do the work.

(continued)

(continued)

❑ I have a high energy level and am willing to use it.

❑ I'm willing to do more than just my job.

❑ I can give instructions and train people.

❑ I can work under pressure and stress.

❑ When things get tough, I can always be counted on.

❑ I'm always willing to take on more responsibility.

❑ I always follow rules and company procedures.

Once you've worked through the preceding exercises and determined which strengths you want to present during the interview, make sure you have good examples of each and begin weaving them into a story for the interviewer.

Your goal should be to have between three and five strengths in your interview answer for the question "What are your major strengths?" And you should have at least three examples of when you've demonstrated each of those strengths. If you don't have three examples for a strength, it can't be considered one of your strengths!

Sample Answer

This response works really well for a person who has little prior work experience related to the job he or she now seeks:

One of my major strengths is my ability to work hard toward a goal. Once I make a decision to accomplish something, it gets done and done well. For example, I graduated from high school four years ago. Many of my friends started working, and others went on to college. At the time, I didn't know what I wanted to do, so furthering my education at that point did not make sense. The jobs I could get at the time didn't excite me, either, so I looked into joining the navy.

I took the ASVAB test and discovered a few things about myself that surprised me. For one thing, I was much better at understanding complex problems than my grades in high school would suggest. I signed up for a three-year hitch that included intensive training in electronics. I worked *hard and graduated in the top 20 percent of my class. I was then assigned to monitor, diagnose, and repair an advanced electronics system that was worth about $20 million. I was promoted several times to the position of Petty Officer and received an honorable discharge after my tour of duty. I now know what I want to do and am prepared to spend extra time learning whatever is needed to do well here.*

Once you begin speaking about one of your strengths, the rest of your response often falls into place naturally, as this sample response illustrates. Remember to provide some proof of your skills, as this respondent did by citing results of navy entrance testing and repeated advancement in a highly responsible position. These specifics about your skills make a difference.

Question #7: "Why Should I Hire You?"

"I need a job so that I can pay my child support" isn't the answer the interviewer wants to hear—even though this might be the truth.

Yes, this is another self-promotion question. Most of the people who have trouble answering this question are uncomfortable with self-promotion questions and think a good answer will make them sound like they're bragging about themselves. One thing is for certain in the interview: If you don't give an interviewer reasons for hiring you, he won't.

The key to answering this question is to understand what employers want from their workforces. No matter what type of work you're seeking, every employer wants the same basic things from you. You have to verbally show the interviewer that you can meet the company's needs. To help you do this, here's a little exercise.

Exercise

How do you plan to show the employer you possess each of the following desired work traits? Use the blank space to make a couple of notes to help you remember.

Employers Want People Who...	How Will You Show You Have What the Employer Wants?
Create a profit and are productive.	_____
Don't create personnel problems.	_____
Do more than just the job.	_____
Fit in with coworkers.	_____
Possess relevant education and training.	_____
Can solve work-related problems.	_____
Demonstrate a little uniqueness.	_____
Will be loyal to the company.	_____
Possess relevant skills and work experience.	_____
Will stay in the position for a reasonable time.	_____
Can learn new skills quickly.	_____
Are reliable and have good attendance.	_____
Display a history of success and achievement.	_____
Are motivated and ambitious.	_____
Are career minded with an interest in the field.	_____
Show an interest in the company.	_____

The following sample answer tries to incorporate as many of the traits an employer wants as possible—in about 30 to 60 seconds.

Sample Answer

You should hire me because I don't need to be trained and have a proven track record. I have more than 15 years of education and experience related to this position. More than six of those years have been in management positions similar to the one available here. In my last position, I was promoted three times in the six years I was there. I most recently had responsibility for supervising a staff of 15 and a warehousing operation that processed more than $30 million in materials a year. In the last two years, I managed a 40 percent increase in volume processed with only a 6 percent increase in expenses. I am hardworking and have earned a reputation as a dependable and creative problem solver. The opportunities here excite me. My substantial experience with other employers will help me in knowing how to approach similar situations here. I am also willing to ask questions and accept advice from others. This willingness will be an important factor in taking advantage of what has already been accomplished here.

Now try to build an answer for yourself, and when doing so, remember one thing about employers: They like comparative numbers and quantifiable results. If you have numbers to present (dollar amounts, lengths of time, percentages, sizes, volume, frequency, duration, and so on) in your answers and the other applicants don't, you win the interviewing game.

Question #8: "What Are Your Plans for the Future?"

Employers want a return on investment in hiring, and two of the best ways for them to get it are to ensure that the people they hire will stay with the company for a reasonable period of time and that those people have a serious interest in the field or the job. Future-oriented questions give interviewers some insight into what motivates a person to work and why that person decided to apply to this company.

Most employers want long-term relationships. Any type of answer that gives the interviewer the slightest clue that you're not interested in a long-term relationship with the company is a bad answer.

To build a good answer, you also need to realize that the interviewer is really asking you six questions in one:

- Will you stay with the company?

- Do your life and work plans match the company's needs and goals?

- Do you have career ambitions?

- Do you have an understanding of the field, not just the job?

- Do you think ahead or just live in the present?

- Are you willing to do whatever is necessary to advance?

As always, your best approach is an honest one. Don't reveal negative information, but be prepared to respond to the employer's concerns in a direct and positive way. Which issues are of concern to an employer depends on your background.

For example:

- You have had a high salary for a position in the past. (Will you be happy with the salary offered now?)

- Your situation suggests you might want to start a family soon. (Will you quit or cut your hours to raise children?)

- You have a history of leaving jobs after a short period of time. (Why won't you leave this one, too?)

- You just moved to the area or appear to be a temporary or transient resident. (Will you stay here long?)

- You are more than qualified. (What will keep you from going to a better job as soon as you find one?)

- You haven't displayed the energy and commitment to advance in this job. (Will you ramp up to the needed level of energy and drive?)

- You appear to have some other reason to eventually become dissatisfied. (Will this reason be a problem?)

Any of these factors, and others, can be of concern to an employer. If your situation presents an obvious problem, be ready with the standard Three-Step Process for answering problem interview questions from chapter 1. Assure the employer that this is precisely the organization you want to stay with, grow with, and do well with for many years to come.

Sample Answer #1

This response works well for a younger person or one just entering a new career:

I realize I need to establish myself in this field and am eager to get started. I've thought about what I want to do and am very sure my skills are the right ones for doing well in this career. For example, I am good at dealing with people. In one position, I provided services to more than 1,000 different people a week. During the 18 months I was there, I served more than 72,000 customers and not once was a complaint filed against me. In fact, I was often complimented on the attention I gave them. There I learned that I enjoy public contact, and I am delighted at the idea of taking on this position for that reason. I want to learn more about this business and grow with it. As my contributions and value to the organization increase, I hope to be considered for more responsible positions.

The employer wants to know that you will stay in this position for an acceptable amount of time and work hard. This response addresses the concern that you are new to the industry (and could possibly wash out of it quickly) and helps the employer feel more comfortable. (Note that this response could be based on work experiences gained in a fast-food job!)

Sample Answer #2

This response works for a person with gaps in work history or various short-term jobs:

I've had a number of jobs [or one, or have been unemployed for a long time], and I have learned to value a good, stable position. The variety of my experiences is an asset because I have learned so many things I can now apply to this position. I am looking for a position where I can settle in, work hard, and stay put.

This response would be even better if it were a bit longer and included some proof of the job seeker's skills. The ideal place to introduce a story would be right before the last sentence.

Sample Answer #3

This answer will work in just about any situation:

I understand how difficult, costly, and time-consuming it must be to recruit, interview, and hire someone from the outside. I'm looking for more than just a job. I want to develop a career with this company and build a long-term working relationship. I want to learn everything I can about this position and begin finding out what I need to know to move up in the company/department. I'm ambitious and plan on working hard here. I really want to advance, so I'm willing to do whatever is needed. If it's more education or on-the-job training, I'll get it. From what I know about the company and what I've learned from you during the interview, as long as I'm being productive for you and I'm learning new things, I can't see why either of us would want to part ways.

With this style of answer, the interviewee lets the interviewer know he or she understands the questions behind the question and shows that the interviewee is motivated to do good work, stay in the company, and advance.

Question #9: "What Are Your Pay Expectations?"

"Whatever's fair," "Whatever you think I'm worth," and "I'll take what's offered" aren't good answers to this question. Answers like these rob you of an opportunity to negotiate for higher starting pay.

In Daniel Porot's book *101 Salary Secrets*, he calls this the most important three minutes of the interview—and is that ever the truth. Think about it for a minute. This question is the reason for you being in the interview in the first place. Unless you're planning to work for free, your goal should be to get as much as you possibly can.

Here's an example of the importance of answering this question well. If a 21-year-old worker starts out making $20,000 per year versus $21,000 per year, and that person works for 50 years and gets standard raises, the extra $1,000 starting pay translates into around $113,000 of extra income that person wouldn't have had if he or she went for the $20,000 offer. Is it worth more than $100,000 to learn how to answer pay-expectation questions? Of course!

How you handle this question is not only a major factor in getting a job offer, it's also important to your job satisfaction. People who feel they're underpaid don't put in extra effort and just do the minimum amount of work to keep the job. If you're one of those folks, you can count on being unhappy with the job, seriously discouraged when it comes time for raises and promotions, the first person let go when a layoff comes, and more likely to get fired or quit without having another job in hand.

So what do you need to do to prepare for this question? First, determine what the local labor market pays for someone with your skills, abilities, education, and experience. This means you need to do local labor market research to find out what you're worth.

Your second task is to do an in-depth budget analysis to determine what your liabilities are (what you need to pay the bills), then add 30 percent and factor in the cost of health insurance for you and your family. This is your lowball figure. If the offer isn't at least this amount, you need to keep looking, begin negotiating, or find a rich relative to supplement your income.

Finally, you need to learn how to negotiate. Salary-negotiation techniques are covered in chapter 8.

Remember, the employer wants you to name a number that can be compared to a figure the company has in mind. Suppose that the employer is looking to pay someone $36,000 a year. If you say you were hoping for $40,000, you will probably be eliminated from consideration. The employer will be afraid that, if you took the job, you might not stay. On the other hand, if you say you would take $29,000, one of two things could happen:

1. You could get hired at $29,000 a year, making that response the most expensive two seconds in your entire life.

2. The employer might keep looking for someone else, because you must be worth only $36,000 and the employer is looking for someone worth more.

This question is designed to help the employer either eliminate you from consideration or save money at your expense. You could get lucky and guess the salary the employer had in mind, but the stakes are too high for me to recommend that approach.

At this stage, instead of answering directly, try to put off discussion of pay until you are sure a real offer is being made and the question of salary is not just part of a screening process. Employers often use discussions of pay in an initial interview to screen people out. Because you aren't likely to get a firm job offer in a first interview, your objective should be to create a positive impression and not be rejected.

Avoid getting nailed down. There are many different ways to effectively deal with the question without giving a direct response. The following are some things you could say:

- "Are you making me a job offer?" (A bit corny, yes, but you just might be surprised at the result.)

- "What salary range do you pay for positions with similar requirements?"

- "I'm very interested in the position, and my salary would be negotiable."

- "Tell me what you have in mind for the salary range."

- "I need to hear more about the position before I can come up with a solid number."

- "I've researched the pay and compensation for people with my skills and experience in this area and found that the low side is $30,000, the high side is $40,000, and that benefits varied. How close are these figures to what you have budgeted for this position?"

Sometimes the pay expectation question comes in the form of a bracket.

Our pay scale for this position ranges from $30,000 to $40,000. Is that acceptable?

You need to be careful here. If you agree to this amount, you may end up with the $30,000 instead of the $40,000. If 10 grand isn't important to you, just say "that's fine." But you might want to consider splitting the bracket by saying something like this:

I was thinking somewhere between $35,000 and $45,000. It seems like we're in the same ballpark, doesn't it?

With this answer, you're at least giving yourself a shot at a little higher starting wage. Check out chapter 8 for more on salary negotiations.

Question #10: "What Will Your Former Employers or Coworkers Say About You?"

Interviewers know that one of the best ways to predict new employee success is to check references, yet a myth that permeates the labor market is that employers rarely check references. The reality is that reference and background checks are performed by more than 90 percent of employers—and that more than 90 percent of employers divulge some form of information.

Your goal in answering this question is to make sure there is agreement between what your former employers, coworkers, teachers, and so on say about you and what you say about yourself.

There are four keys to answering reference-oriented questions:

- Know what everyone who might be contacted will say about you.

- Anticipate the kinds of information that will be sought in a background check.

- Never ask anyone to lie for you.

- Don't hesitate or hedge when answering reference questions.

REFERENCE-CHECKING WORKSHEET

To help you build a better answer, honestly evaluate what you think your former employer(s) and coworker(s) will say about you based on these 24 common reference-checking points.

E—Excellent   G—Good   F—Fair   P—Poor

1. Is punctual ____	12. Accepts instruction ____
2. Has good attendance ____	13. Possesses relevant writing skills ____
3. Accepts overtime ____	14. Possesses relevant math skills ____
4. Does job until it's right ____	15. Shows good moral character ____
5. Is honest ____	16. Produces high work quality ____
6. Has job/technical knowledge ____	17. Completes high work quantity ____
7. Displays interpersonal skills ____	18. Demonstrates company loyalty ____
8. Accepts criticism ____	19. Does extra work ____
9. Respects supervisors ____	20. Has a history of success ____
10. Has ability to instruct ____	
11. Gets ideas across ____	

(continued)

(continued)

21. Has advancement potential	____	23. Needs little supervision	____
22. Learns quickly	____	24. Shows leadership skills	____

Don't allow yourself to get blindsided with a bad reference check! Contact your former employers and coworkers. Tell them the type of job you're applying for, give them the name of the company you're applying to, and ask them to tell you what they'll say about you if asked—even if it's not good. You can always prepare to counter a negative statement if you know it's coming.

If you were fired from you previous job or resigned under pressure, you can often negotiate what will be said to a prospective employer. Lots of successful people have had personality conflicts with previous employers. If these conflicts are presented openly and in the best light possible, many interviewers are likely to understand. It might also be wise to get a written letter of reference, particularly from a not-too-enthusiastic former employer. Such an employer is rarely brave enough to write you a totally negative letter. The letter might be enough to satisfy a potential employer. Larger organizations often don't allow employees to give references; if you are worried about a negative reference, this rule might be a great relief to you. Call your former employers and find out their policies.

If you think your ex-boss won't say nice things about you, find someone who will. Your alternative references should come from people who have seen the quality of your work and your interpersonal skills daily.

Sample Answer #1

My last boss didn't share my vision of the best practices for that position, so you might not get a great picture of my work and interpersonal skills from her. But, if you call the other members of my assembly team, I know you'll get a more balanced picture. Would you like me to give you any of their numbers or contact information?

Interviewers often appreciate an honest response to this question. If you failed in a job, telling the truth is the best policy. Tell it like it was, but *do not* be too critical of your old boss. If you do, it will make you sound like a person who blames others and does not accept responsibility. If you were partly at fault, admit it, but quickly take the opportunity to explain what you learned from the experience.

Sample Answer #2

My three former employers will all say that I work hard, am very reliable, and am loyal. The reason I left my previous job, however, is the result of what I can only call a mismatch. It was unfortunate, but I decided that it was time I parted with my former employer. You can call and get a reference, but I thought it only fair to tell you. I still respect my ex-boss and am grateful for the experience I gained at that job. While there, I received several promotions, but as my authority increased, the divide in shared vision also increased. Our styles were just not the same. I had no idea the problem was so serious because I was fully involved in my work. That was my error, and I have since learned to pay more attention to certain interpersonal matters.

This response could be strengthened by the introduction of related positive skills being further developed along with an example that includes some proof to support them.

Question #11: "How Does Your Previous Experience Relate to This Job?"

This is another direct question that requires a direct response. If you have created a good impression up to this point, your response to this question is especially important. It requires you to overcome any weaknesses your background might present when you are compared to other job seekers.

Here are some typical stumbling blocks:

- You are just out of school and have limited experience in this career.
- This is your first job, or you have not worked for a period of time.
- Your prior work experience does not present an obvious match for the tasks required in this job.
- Your previous level of responsibility was lower or higher than this job requires.
- You have had several jobs, but no clear career direction.
- You do not have the education or other credentials many other applicants might have.

Lead with your strengths. If it is obvious that other job seekers might have more education, more years of experience, or whatever qualifications you lack, acknowledge that, and then present your strengths. Use the standard Three-Step Process from chapter 1 in answering this problem question.

To prepare for this question, take a look at your list of transferable skills and see which of them best match up to the demands of the job for which you're applying.

You can also brainstorm by using a comparative-tasks analysis form. On the left side of the form, list the duties, responsibilities, skills, and experience needed to do the job. On the right side, look back through your life, work, military, and educational experiences for instances when you've done something similar and look for linkage and transferability.

TRANSFERABLE SKILLS WORKSHEET

Skills and Abilities Needed	Examples of When You Used These
_____	_____
_____	_____
_____	_____
_____	_____

Sample Answer #1

As you know, I have just completed an intensive program studying information technology. In addition, I have more than three years of work experience in a variety of business settings. That work experience includes managing a small business during the absence of the owner. I learned to handle money there and do a variety of basic accounting tasks. I also inventoried and organized products worth more than $600,000. These experiences helped me understand the importance of good information technology systems in a business setting.

Although I am a recent information technology graduate, my previous business experience allows me to understand how to use what I have learned in practical and effective ways. My educational experience was very thorough, and I have more than 300 hours of interactive computer time as part of my coursework. Because I am new to this career, I plan to work harder and will spend extra time as needed to meet deadlines.

This response emphasizes transferable skills (knowledge of accounting procedures) and self-management skills (meeting deadlines and working hard). This emphasis is necessary to counter a lack of previous work experience in the information technology area. In this situation, what the candidate learned in school is also very important and should be emphasized as the equivalent of "real" work.

Sample Answer #2

In my previous position, I used many of the same skills that are needed to do this job well. Even though it was in a different industry, managing a business requires the types of organizational and supervisory skills that I possess. Over the past seven years, I guided my region to become one of the most profitable in our company. Sales expanded an average of 30 percent per year during the years I worked there, and profits rose at a similar rate. Because this is a mature company, such performance is highly unusual. I received two promotions during those seven years and rose to the management level quickly. I was later told that no one had previously achieved this kind of advancement. I am now seeking a challenge in a smaller, growth-oriented company such as yours. I feel my experience and contacts have prepared me for this step in my career.

This response acknowledges that the previous career field differed from the one now being considered but emphasizes prior achievements and success. Accomplishing this level of success requires the use of all sorts of skills. The response also includes the motivation to move on to the challenge of a smaller organization.

Question #12: "Why Did You Select This Line of Work, Career Path, or Field?"

Interviewees who respond to this question by saying "I just lucked into it" miss a golden opportunity to convince the employer that they are a low-risk hire. Employers know that people willing to invest time and energy in making a career decision usually stay on the job longer, are more satisfied with their jobs, and are more loyal to the company.

This is a fairly simple question to answer because all you need to do is tell the truth. Did you take an interest, abilities, or any other type of vocational evaluation or career decision-making test? Did you know someone who performed this kind of work and you liked it? Did you talk with a career counselor or use a self-help book on career selection? Or do your skills, educational experiences, and personality traits (self-management skills) match up to the job?

Sample Answer #1

An experienced manager or a sharp office worker could use the following type of response.

> *I've spent a lot of time considering various careers, and I think that this is the best area for me. The reason is that this career requires many of my strongest skills. For example, my abilities in analyzing and solving problems are two of the skills I enjoy using most. In a previous position, I would often become aware of a problem no one had noticed and develop a solution. In one situation, I suggested a plan that resulted in reducing customer returns of leased equipment by 15 percent. That might not sound like much, but the result was an increase in retained leases of more than $250,000 a year. The plan cost about $100 to implement.*

This response uses the Prove It technique nicely.

Sample Answer #2

> *I wanted to make sure I pursued a career that fit my personality, education, and skills, so I took a personality test called the Myers-Briggs Type Indicator and found out my code is ENFP. One of the job groups that goes with this code is marketing. Then I took an interest test, and it showed one of my highest interest areas as being entrepreneurial. Marketing, advertising, and promotional occupations are where I belong.*

Be careful with this approach! If you haven't taken the tests, don't try to bluff your way through. A good interviewer will ask you for more specific information only a person who had taken the tests would be able to answer.

Question #13: "Could You Tell Me About Your Personal Situation?"

A good interviewer will rarely ask this question so directly. If this question is asked this directly, simply respond by asking the interviewer something like, "What is it you would like to know?" In this way, you show the interviewer that you have nothing to hide without immediately giving anything away. More often, interviewers use casual and friendly conversation to get the information they want. In most cases, the interviewer is digging for information that would indicate you are unstable or undependable.

Other issues might be of concern to an employer as well. Often these are based on beliefs the person has about people with certain characteristics. These beliefs are often irrelevant (and some might seem to be in bad taste or even illegal), but if the employer wonders whether you can be depended upon, dealing with these doubts is in your best interest. Be aware that even your casual conversation should always avoid reference to a potential problem area. In responding to a question about your personal situation, be friendly and positive. Your objective is to give employers the answers that they need to have and nothing more. See chapter 5 for guidelines on handling illegal questions.

Sample Answers

The following responses address the personal issues that employers are most often concerned about.

- Young children at home:

  "I have two children, both in school. Child care is no problem because they stay with a good friend."

- Single head of household:

  "I'm not married and have two children at home. It is very important to me to have a steady income, so I make sure child care is not a problem."

- Young and single:

  "I'm not married, and if I should marry, that would not change my plans for a full-time career."

- Just moved here:

  "I've decided to settle here in Depression Gulch permanently. I've rented an apartment, and the six moving vans are unloading there now."

- Relatives, upbringing:

  "I am one of three children. Both of my parents still live within an hour's flight from here, and I see them several times a year."

- Leisure time:

  "My time is family-centered when I'm not working. I'm also active in several community organizations and spend at least some time each week in church activities."

All of these responses could be expanded on, but they should give you an idea of the types of approaches you can take with your own answers. The message you want to give is that your personal situation will not hurt your ability to work. If your personal life does disrupt your work, expect most employers to lose patience quickly. It is not their problem, nor should it be.

100 Other Frequently Asked Interview Questions

The following list presents questions most often asked by interviewers and recruiters. Although some of the questions might not apply to your situation, they give you a good idea of the types of questions a trained interviewer will ask you in an interview. Look over the list and check any that could be hard for you to answer well. Then practice coming up with positive answers for those problem questions using the Three-Step Process for answering interview questions.

1. Are you involved in lifelong learning? If so, what are you doing?

2. What person has had the most influence on your life?

3. Can you tell me about a time when you had to help a coworker that you didn't get along with?

4. What really motivates you?

5. What jobs have you held? How did you obtain your previous jobs?

6. What courses did you like best in school? Least? Why?

7. Do you still keep in touch with former bosses or coworkers?

8. What percentage of your school expenses did you earn or get scholarships for? How?

9. How did you spend your vacations while in school?

10. Have you ever been fired or asked to resign?

11. Do you feel that you have received good general training?

12. What qualifications do you have that make you feel that you will be successful in this field?

13. Have you ever been elected to a leadership position in a club or professional association?

14. How long have you been looking for work?

15. Has a supervisor or coworker ever challenged one of your decisions? How did you deal with that?

16. Do you volunteer for community organizations?

17. What level of involvement do you have in any professional organizations?

18. If you were starting school all over again, what would you do differently?

19. What is the most useful piece of advice or criticism you've ever received?

20. Do you prefer any specific geographic location? Why?

21. What type of family situation are you currently in (married, kids, single, divorced, and so on)?

22. How much money do you hope to earn at age _____?

23. Why did you decide to go to the school you attended?

24. How did you rank in your graduating class in high school? Other schools?

25. Did you participate in extracurricular activities while in school? Was the time you devoted to them worth it? Why?

26. What do you think determines a person's progress in a good company?

27. What personal characteristics are necessary for success in your chosen field?

28. What do you like about this type of work?

29. What types of books or magazines do you read? What was the last book you read or movie you went to?

30. Tell me about your home life growing up.

31. Are you looking for a permanent or temporary job?

32. Do you prefer working with others or by yourself?

33. What types of people are your best friends?

34. What kind of boss do you prefer?

35. What are some values you want from the job other than money?

36. Can you take instructions without feeling upset?

37. Will you tell me a story? (Interviewers might ask this question to see how you'll interpret it. Be sure your story is about your career and shows that you are the right person for the job.)

38. How did you prepare for this interview?

39. How did previous employers treat you?

40. What have you learned from some of the jobs you have held?

41. What qualities do you most admire in people?

42. What interests you about our product or service?

43. Can you tell me about your military experiences?

44. Have you ever changed your major field of interest? Why?

45. What's the worst mistake you've made, and what did you learn from it?

46. Have you ever had a clash with a coworker, supervisor, customer, or vendor? How did you handle the situation?

47. Do you feel you have done the best work you are capable of?

48. Can you give me an example of when you've been the most creative?

49. What do you know about opportunities in this field?

50. Have you ever thought you might be overqualified for this position?

51. Describe your perfect job.

52. What's the toughest work-related problem you've had to face?

53. Can you tell me about a time when you've trained or mentored someone?

54. How long will it take you to start making a real contribution to the company?

55. Describe a difficult decision you had to make and tell me how you made up your mind.

56. Would you go back to the company that laid you off if you were given the chance?

57. How old were you when you became self-supporting?

58. Describe what you consider to be a typical work day?

59. Did you enjoy school? What did you like about it the best and least?

60. Can you give me an example of a time when you've had to work collaboratively with a team?

61. Describe a time when you've had to work without direct supervision.

62. What did you like least and most about your last job, supervisors, and coworkers?

63. What type of interests do you have outside of work?

64. Are you willing to take calculated risks?

65. Define cooperation.

66. Can you give me an example of when you've done extra work to get ahead or to help out the company or a coworker?

67. What job functions did you like performing the most and least?

68. Do you have an analytical mind?

69. What do you think the role of an employee is?

70. How would you rate your own physical condition?

71. What jobs have you enjoyed the most and the least?

72. Have you had any serious illness or injury that could stop you from doing the job?

73. Are you willing to relocate if it becomes necessary in this job?

74. What job in our company would you choose to have if you were entirely free to do so?

75. Are you tolerant of different races, religions, cultures, and lifestyles?

76. What types of on-the-job training have you completed?

77. If you could change one thing about yourself, what would it be?

78. What types of people seem to rub you the wrong way?

79. Can you describe your personality in 10 words?

80. Have you ever tutored a peer or provided training to someone?

81. How was your last performance evaluation?

82. What unique abilities do you have?

83. What job in our company do you want to work toward?

84. Do you prefer working for a large company or a small company? Why?

85. What is your idea of how this industry operates today?

86. Do you like to travel?

87. Are you willing to accept overtime work?

88. What kind of work interests you?

89. What are the disadvantages of your chosen field?

90. Do you think that employers should consider grades? Why or why not?

91. How do you handle criticism?

92. Can you give me an example of when you've failed and how you dealt with it?

93. Would you be willing to take a drug test in the next hour?

94. What have you done that shows initiative?

95. How would you define success?

96. Did you have a good relationship with your last boss? How would you describe it?

97. Can you tell me about a time when you had to work under a great deal of pressure?

98. How many days of work [or school] did you miss last year?

99. How many different jobs have you interviewed for in your latest search?

100. When are you available to start? [This is the question you want to be asked the most!]

Key Points: Chapter 4

- Prepare yourself for an interview by thinking through your answers to the most common interview questions.

- Answer difficult questions honestly, but always present yourself in a positive light.

- Use your responses to the interview questions to emphasize how your skills fit the employer's needs and reassure the interviewer that you are the best choice for this position.

Chapter 5

Handling Tough Interview Questions and Unusual Situations

The odds are very high that you could be eliminated from consideration for jobs based on your answer (or, more likely, your lack of a good answer) to one or more of the interview questions or issues we bring up in this chapter. None of us is perfect. We all have things about ourselves and our past that could be or will be a problem for some employers. You might have "too much" or "too little" education or training or gaps in your work history; you might be "too old" or "too young" or have other characteristics that concern some employers. Some of these things you can't change, but it is your responsibility to make these matters less of an issue. In other words, your job during the interview is to reduce the employer's perception of you as a hiring risk and make him or her like you, even if there's been something negative in your past personal, employment, or educational history.

We mentioned earlier that 90 percent of all people who get interviews do not, according to surveys of employers, do a good job in answering one or more interview questions. These problem questions vary for each person and depend on the individual's situation. A job seeker's inability to answer these problem questions is a very big obstacle in the job search and has kept many good people from getting jobs they are perfectly capable of handling. They didn't get those jobs because they failed to convince employers that they had the skills and other characteristics to do the job. In many cases, they gave employers a sense that there was an unresolved problem and left a question mark in those employers' minds. Employers would much rather deal with a known negative than worry about an unknown.

One of the difficulties with problem questions is that employers often do not ask these questions in a clear way, or do not ask them at all. For example, if you live a long distance from an employer's job site, the interviewer might wonder why you would be willing to commute daily to such a distant location. His concern might be that you would leave once you found a job closer to home. The interviewer might never directly ask you about working so far away from home, so you would not have the opportunity to address his or her concern, and that job is likely to go to someone else. It's not fair, but that's the way it is.

So the issue here is not your ability to just *do* the job; rather the issue is your ability to communicate clearly that you *can* and *will* do the job. This chapter helps you quickly identify problem questions an employer might pose about your particular situation and helps you handle them in truthful and positive ways.

Dealing with Illegal Questions

Technically, America is a free country. Our Constitution gives all of us the right of free speech, including the right of an employer to ask inappropriate questions. Employers can ask almost anything they want in an interview or on an application. They can ask offensive questions, personal questions, and even just plain dumb questions.

The problem arises when employers hire one person over another based on answers to certain questions that require disclosure of criteria such as race, gender, or religion. Such hiring practices are illegal, although it is very difficult to prove that an employer has actually done this after the fact. The truth is that some employers base their hiring decisions on things that should not be issues at all, such as age, religious affiliation, weight, family status, physical beauty, and race or ethnic background.

If you are faced with such questions, you have to ask yourself whether you still want the job. If you do, you'll have to let the employer know you will be a good choice by answering the question in the most positive way possible.

There are situations (thankfully, very rare) in which an interviewer's questions are totally offensive. They might be offensive in the way they are asked or because of the type of questions they are. If that is the case, you should consider that you might not want to work for such a person. You just might, in this sort of situation, tactfully tell that employer what you think of him or her. You might also consider reporting that employer to the authorities.

Know the Laws Protecting You from Discrimination

Two major laws come into play in cases of hiring discrimination:

- Title VII of the Civil Rights Act, which was enacted in 1964 and is still very much in effect, makes discrimination on the basis of race, gender, religion, or national origin illegal in hiring decisions.

- The Americans with Disabilities Act, which was passed in 1990 and put into effect in 1992, requires that employers provide an equal opportunity for an individual with a disability to participate in a job application process and to be considered for a job.

> **Tip:** *If you think that you have been discriminated against in the job hiring process, visit the U.S. Equal Employment Opportunity Commission Web site at www.eeoc.gov. This Web site contains guidelines for determining whether discrimination has occurred and instructions for filing a complaint.*

A specific job might require an answer to some questions that appear to be illegal for other jobs. For example, firefighters need to be in good physical condition because they might be required to climb a ladder while carrying 100 or more pounds. Therefore, strength and health-related questions are acceptable in interviews for firefighters. Bartenders need to be at least 21 years old, so the interviewer can ask about age when interviewing a bartender. These are examples of legitimate job-related questions that an employer can ask when interviewing people for these jobs. In general, an employer is not allowed to ask for or consider information that is not related to a person's ability to do the job.

A Few Options for Handling Illegal Questions

How you deal with a potentially illegal question can be just as important as the answer you have to the question. As an example, if the interviewer asks "Are you planning to start a family soon?"—an obviously illegal question in most instances—you have some decisions to make. The following are some of your options.

Tell the Interviewer the Question Is Illegal

You can let the person know that you think the question is illegal or out of bounds:

Do you realize that this question is considered an illegal question and that I don't have to answer it?

The interviewer will probably be put on the defensive and might see you as someone who will be a potential problem on the work site.

Ask About the Question's Relevance

You can ask about the relevance of the question:

Can you tell me how this question and my answer to it have any bearing on my ability to do the job?

This is a little less harsh but still puts the interviewer on notice that he or she might have stepped over the line. However, you're not refusing to answer. You just need some clarification.

Reassure the Interviewer

You can show them that you understand why the question might be asked.

It seems like you must have had issues with someone who got pregnant and quit in the past? If what you're asking is "do I plan to leave this job in the next year," the answer is no. In fact, I plan to continue working while raising a family.

This approach lets the interviewer know that you understand the rationale behind the question and doesn't put him or her on the defensive.

Turn the Negative into a Positive

Begin by considering why an employer might be concerned about you or your situation. Is it possible the employer thinks that you would be less reliable, less productive, or in some other way less capable of doing the job because of his or her misconceptions about your situation? If so, practice an answer that helps the interviewer understand why the perceived problem will not be an issue.

For example, if you have young children at home (an issue, by the way, that men are rarely asked about), it is to your advantage to mention that you have excellent child care and don't expect any problems. In addition, look for a way to present your "problem" as an advantage. Perhaps you could say that your additional responsibilities make it even more important for you to be well-organized, a skill that you have developed over many years and fully expect to apply in the new job. In this way, you turn your disadvantage into an advantage.

The Turtling Technique

Like a turtle on its back, a problem is a problem only if you leave it that way. By turning it over ("turtling" it), you can often turn a perceived disadvantage into an advantage. Take a look at the following examples to understand what we mean:

- **Too old:** "I am a stable worker who requires very little training. I have been dependable all my life, and I am at a point in my career where I don't plan on changing jobs. I still have 10 years of working until I plan on retiring. How long does the average employment last here?"

- **Too young:** "I don't have any bad work habits to break, so I can be quickly trained to do things the way you want. I plan on working hard to get established."

You can use the turtling technique on most problem questions. Just turn what some might see as a negative into a positive.

Common Areas Covered by Illegal Questions

If an employer can support the need to ask an illegal question, the question is no longer illegal. Even attorneys have trouble deciphering when a question is illegal. The following are some of the more common types of questions untrained interviewers might ask that could be considered illegal or out of bounds.

- Questions related to citizenship, birthplace, family's nationality or citizenship, or language spoken at home.

- Questions that specifically inquire about your date of birth, your age, or the ages of your family members.

- Questions about arrests (not convictions), criminal charges, or your family criminal history.

- Questions relating to disabilities, general health, treatment for alcoholism or drug abuse, medications currently being taken, hospitalizations for illnesses, and worker's compensation.

- Questions about marital status, maiden name, ancestry of a spouse, number of children, preference of Mrs. or Miss.

- Questions about social organizations or clubs, political movements, or associations to which you belong or are affiliated with.

- Questions about race or ethnicity. (These are always out of bounds.)

- Questions about your religious affiliations, religious holidays you celebrate, and organizations you contribute to.

- Questions about your type of residence, home ownership, leasing, renting, and who's living with you.

- Questions about your financial status, banking information, and credit card and loan information.

- Questions about gender, sexual preference, information about a significant other.

Answer Open-Ended Questions Effectively

Employers want to get the information they need to make a safe, profitable hiring decision. You, the candidate, want some privacy and a fair chance to be considered based on your work-related merits. Open-ended interview questions generally achieve both goals.

For instance, instead of an employer asking "Are you living with anyone?" she might phrase the question as "Do you foresee any situations that would prevent you from traveling or relocating?" The employer might want to know whether you have any limitations regarding work schedule or whether you have roots in the area that will encourage you to stay. The less direct question allows you to decide what information about your private life applies to the job at hand. Of course, if you are not prepared for such a question, you could provide information that might damage your chances for getting the job.

Employers often want to know the details of your personal situation for legitimate reasons. They want to be sure that you can be depended on to stay on the job and work hard. Your task in the interview is to provide information indicating that, yes, you can be counted on to do the job. If you don't get that idea across, you will probably not be considered for the job.

Refer to chapter 1 for details on the Three-Step Process you can use to answer any question, including open-ended questions.

Help with Specific Problem Situations

This section deals with issues most people experience and that are often legitimate issues for an employer to explore. These issues include things such as gaps in your employment or being fired from a previous job. Employers are more likely to ask about these matters in a direct way.

Gaps in Your Work History

Some of the most accomplished people we know have been out of work at one time or another. About one out of five people in the workforce experiences unemployment each year. Unemployment is not a sin, and most bosses have experienced it themselves.

Employers realize it's not unusual for a person to be unemployed for some length of time. As a rule of thumb, the higher paid you are, the longer it will take you to find another job. Although there are "average lengths of unemployment" figures, about six months is considered normal. If you've been unemployed for longer than six months, you need to prepare for the question "Why have you been unemployed so long?"

Some people advocate trying to cover the fact that you have a job gap by using a traditional resume writing technique of writing "20XX to Present" when referring to your most recent job, which makes it look as if you are still employed. If you use this trick, however, realize that it puts you in an uncomfortable position right away. One of the first things you will have to do in the interview is explain that this is not actually the case. Some employers will assume you are misrepresenting other facts about your situation as well—not a good impression for you to create. From this point forward, the interviewer might not believe what you say and will use more probing interview techniques to ferret out the truth. This puts you on the hot seat a lot more often—someplace you don't want to be.

It is more acceptable to use a similar technique with past employment gaps. Refer to dates in years rather than months. This is still accurate but hides short job gaps. Of course, if pressed, give the exact dates without hesitation.

If you have a legitimate reason for major gaps, such as going to school or having a child, tell the interviewer in a matter-of-fact way; don't apologize or act embarrassed about it. You could, however, add details about a related activity you did during that period that would strengthen your qualifications for the job at hand. This kind of detail reinforces that you are not out of touch with what the employer needs.

With the question "Why have you been unemployed so long?" the interviewer wants to know two things: the reason for your unemployment and what you did with that time. If what you did during that period of time helped you prepare for a new job or was used to fix a problem that affected your work performance, you get a few extra points. The following is an example of how a person who's been unemployed for a lengthy time might respond to a job gap question.

> *I was laid off from Tech Met nearly 18 months ago. Since then I've been taking CAD courses at Ivy Tech, maintaining a 3.4 average, and also taking care of my elderly parents. I'm almost done with my CAD certification and my parents are in a nursing home where they receive full-time care. Now everything's in order, and I'm ready for a new career.*

If, by chance, you're someone who just sat idly for longer than six months, contact your local One-Stop Career Center (www.servicelocator.org) so that they can ask you some questions about your situation and help you build an acceptable reason for being unemployed for so long.

Being Fired

If you've just been fired, there's still hope for you! More than 4 million people are fired annually, so you're far from being alone. Virtually all of them have found new work—and so will you.

If you were fired for just cause, you need to learn from the experience and change your behavior or consider another career. Terminations can seriously hurt your chances of getting a new job. In some cases, employers are afraid that you will be a problem for them. However, in most cases, job seekers themselves do more harm to their chances of finding a new job than being fired.

Know How to Explain Your Situation

If you don't know how to explain your situation, you won't do well in interviews. Job seekers too often leave potential employers wondering just what happened at the last job and assuming the worst. Leaving an employer with the thought that you are hiding something is a bad way to make a good impression.

Many employers say they will not hire someone unless they know why the person left his or her last job. They want to be sure that a job seeker is not a potential problem employee. You will definitely have to deal with this worry if you want to get hired after having been fired. The good news here is that many employers have been fired themselves. Normally, people in charge alienate some people or have had interpersonal conflicts or other difficult situations—it goes along with being in charge. If you have a reasonable explanation for being fired, many interviewers will understand because they have had similar experiences.

So if you have lost a job, the best policy is to tell the truth. Be certain to avoid saying negative things about yourself or your last employer. Think about how you can put a positive spin on what happened. If you are not a big problem to work with, say so—and explain how you are very good at the things that *this* job requires. Tell the truth about what happened in your past job in an objective way and quickly turn to presenting the skills you have to do the job under discussion.

What the Interviewer Looks for in Your Answer

Interviewer training books tell us that employers are looking for certain information in the applicant's explanation of a termination:

- They want an honest reason for the termination.

- They want to see whether the applicant's answer matches the information they received from reference checks.

- They're looking for indicators of potential problems with the applicant.

- They want to see whether the applicant understands the cause of the behavior that resulted in the termination.

- They look for any actions the applicant has taken to eliminate the problem(s) that caused the termination.

- They want to see how the applicant talks about former employers.

When developing your answer, ask yourself whether your answer addresses most of these points. If it does, you've probably put together an acceptable response. Here are a couple of sample answers for someone who was fired for just cause that address the employer's concerns. Use these to guide yourself to a better answer to the question "Why were you fired, let go, or asked to resign?"

- "I don't think I lived up to my supervisor's expectations. I probably should have communicated with her more to find out what she wanted from me, but I didn't. I actually had to agree with her when she let me go. Not defining my boss's expectations was a mistake I won't make again."

- "I missed too many days of work. It was my fault. I understand the need to be reliable and that my not being at work put an extra load on other people. I can promise you that poor attendance on my part will no longer be a problem. At that time, I had moved into a new house and had more trouble arranging child care than anticipated. I have since arranged for both daily and emergency babysitting and I'm ready to work. I can even work some weekends and overtime if you need me."

> **Caution:** Don't hesitate, evade, or try to throw the blame for your termination anywhere else. If you do, your answer loses credibility.

Negotiate for Better References

One strategy to consider is to negotiate with your previous employer about what he or she will say when giving you a reference. Ask for a written letter of reference, too. These negotiations can help offset a negative past employer who just might have a simple personality conflict with you. This kind of conflict happens a lot, and it doesn't have to hurt you as much as you might think.

You can also get an alternate reference. Although you might have had a conflict with the previous boss, there are likely others at your previous place of employment who thought well of you. You should contact those people to find out what they might say if asked to provide a reference. You should also try to get written recommendations from them.

Changing Careers or Applying Job History Unrelated to Your Current Job Objective

Career changing is a way of life in today's labor market. Cradle-to-grave employment is a thing of the past, and it's estimated that each person will change jobs around 10 times between the ages of 18 and 40 alone. So this issue isn't as important as you might assume. Sure, the interviewer is curious and wants to get to know you better. But if your past experience were a real barrier, you wouldn't have been invited for an interview in the first place. Stick to emphasizing your skills and how they relate to the job you are discussing. For instance, a teacher who wants to become a real estate sales agent could point to her hobby of investing in and fixing up old houses. She could cite superior communication skills and an ability to motivate people like the students in her classroom.

Look up job descriptions for your old jobs and then descriptions for the one you want now, and find skills that are common to both. Then emphasize those skills in your interviews. The work you did in chapter 2 will also help you document the skills and other strengths you have to support your current job objective.

Employers say that career changers need to do the following three things:

- Have sound reasons for making a career change.

- Indicate that they are willing to start at the bottom.

- Relate how what they've done in the past will be relevant in the new job.

The following exercise will help you brainstorm the skills you have that can be applied to a new career. Take a look at your chapter 2 exercises and list 10 of the most dominant and successful skills that you used in your past jobs. Next, make a note of how each skill can transfer to the job for which you are applying.

Dominant Skill Used in Previous Jobs	How Can This Skill Be Used in the New Job?
1. _____	_____
2. _____	_____
3. _____	_____
4. _____	_____
5. _____	_____
6. _____	_____
7. _____	_____
8. _____	_____

9. _____   _____

10. _____   _____

Recently Moved

Employers are often concerned that someone who has recently moved to an area does not have roots there and might soon leave. If you are new to the area, make sure the employer knows you are there to stay. Provide a simple statement that presents you as a stable member of the community rather than someone with a more transient lifestyle. Some tactics you can use to alleviate the employer's fear that you won't be around long are the following:

- Let the interviewer know that you, your spouse, or your kids are enrolled in a local school.

- Inform the interviewer that your spouse or significant other is currently employed or seeking employment in the area.

- Point out that you have signed a lease or are in the process of purchasing a home in the general locale.

- Note that you are a volunteer in one of the community's social service organizations.

- Mention that you have family and friends in the area and that this is one of the reasons you've chosen to move.

Military Experience

It's safe to say that most employers have not had military experience themselves, nor has most of the labor force. Because of this, there are a number of misconceptions about those with military experience. The truth is that military people are just like everyone else, except that they are perhaps just a bit more responsible, mature, and skilled than the average person. A few facts are in order.

- Forty-five percent of the more than 200,000 people coming out of the military each year are under 25 years old and have technical skills.

- Ninety-two percent of active-duty personnel use computers.

- Fifty-one percent use LAN systems.

- Ninety-eight percent are high school graduates.

- Thirty-six percent have college degrees.

- Exiting military are generally in better health than civilians.

These are some of the skills and educational accomplishments most in demand in the civilian world. The problem is that some of the stereotypes of military people work in your favor, whereas some don't. The following are some common problem areas with corresponding suggestions for dealing with these preconceptions in positive ways:

- **Demonstrate how well you can get along with others.** Some people assume military personnel are overly aggressive. Not true, of course, but you can easily handle this stereotype by being friendly. If you think this might be an issue, emphasize community service you have done (in this country and others), the importance of family and friends to you, and things you have done in and outside of the military that helped others.

- **Reassure the employer that you have strong problem-solving skills.** Another common misconception is that military personnel are too likely to follow orders rather than be creative. More and more jobs require the ability to work as part of a self-directed team that is expected to solve problems with creative input from each member. The truth is that the military has been training creative problem solvers for many years. To overcome any negative stereotypes, you simply need to emphasize your problem-solving skills and experiences.

- **Explain why you left and that you have "civilian" skills.** Most people don't realize how large the U.S. military is. Nearly 3 million people are on active duty or in the reserves, and each year more than 300,000 people leave. Be sure to bring up why you left the military in order to put the interviewer's mind at rest that your leaving had nothing to do with the concept of being fired. In most cases, ex-military people have served their country well, have benefited from excellent and expensive training, are more educated and technologically trained than the average person their age, and have had far more management experience and responsibilities than the average job seeker. The fact is that ex-military are among the most talented and dedicated people available. They are people who have worked hard and have a proven track record for getting difficult things done. Your responsibility in the interview is to make sure the employer knows these things about you.

Emphasize job-related and other skills you have that are needed in the civilian job you seek. Give examples of when you used these skills and any results you obtained. Also emphasize that your military experience developed additional qualities that are important to all employers, including discipline, responsibility, and dependability. A few sites you might want to look at for crosswalking your military experience and skills to civilian job skills are these:

- www.careervoyages.gov

- www.military.com

- www.online.onetcenter.org

- www.militaryjobzone.com

- www.vba.va.gov/bln/vre/index.htm

- **Use civilian dress and language.** To reinforce your abilities as a civilian worker, avoid wearing military tiepins, rings, or other military jewelry or indicators. Completely avoid using any military jargon and replace it with terms that civilians use.

- **Stress your exposure to cultural diversity.** Military personnel must interact with a wide range of people from all races, creeds, genders, education levels, ranks, and economic levels. In a global economy, employers seek out the ability to do this. And in a multicultural workforce, former military personnel can create workplace harmony that translates into higher productivity, fewer problems, and increased profits.

Negative References

Most employers contact your previous employers only if you are being seriously considered as a candidate for the job. If you fear that one of your previous employers might not give you a positive reference, here are some things you can do:

- **List someone other than your former supervisor as a reference.** Consider tapping the people who spent the most direct time with you on the job who can attest to the quality and quantity of your work and how you positively interacted with your coworkers. If you were involved with customers, vendors, or other support staff who know of your work, these folks can also be used as positive references to balance out a negative reference from a supervisor.

- **Discuss the issue in advance with your previous employer and nego-tiate what he or she will say.** Even if it's not good, at least you know what that employer is likely to say and can prepare your potential employers in advance.

- **Get a written letter of reference.** In many cases, employers will not give references over the phone or e-mail (or negative references at all) for fear of being sued. Presenting a letter of reference ensures that you know what is said about your performance.

Criminal Record

More than 2 million people are currently locked up, but most will get out someday. If you happen to be one of these people, your interview will be more difficult than most.

In the United States, we are technically innocent until proven guilty. And that is why employers are no longer supposed to consider an arrest record in a hiring decision. Being arrested and being guilty are two different things. Arrests for minor offenses (misdemeanors) are also not supposed to be considered in a hiring decision. The further argument has been that minorities and urban youth are more likely to have arrest records and con-sideration of arrest records in a hiring decision is, therefore, discriminatory.

The reality is often quite different than the law allows for. In reality, some employers will never hire a person who's been arrested or convicted. Ex-offenders and people who have been arrested will probably receive more interview rejection, be discriminated against more often, have to answer some embarrassing questions, have limitations on the type of work they can pursue, and will have to take certain jobs that other nonoffending applicants might not—just to get back into the labor market.

But don't despair. Between 40 and 60 percent of employers say they will hire an ex-offender if he or she

- Has the skill sets that the employer is looking for.

- Is honest and upfront about the crime.

- Is willing to accept responsibility for the crime, not blame anyone else, and not claim "innocence."

- Shows genuine remorse for the damage he or she has caused to others—not just remorse for being caught and imprisoned.

- Is willing to earn his or her way back into the labor market by starting at the bottom.

- Is doing things that show he or she has changed, such as going to school, becoming active with a church, moving away from a crime-ridden neighborhood, volunteering in the community, and so on.

If you have an arrest or conviction record that an employer *does* have a legal right to inquire about (such as a felony conviction), avoid looking for jobs where your record would be a serious factor. An accountant convicted of embezzling should consider changing careers, and a warehouse worker convicted of drug distribution should avoid applying to a warehouse from which pharmaceuticals are shipped. Even if either of these people did get one of these jobs by concealing his or her criminal history, that person could be fired at any time in the future when it's discovered. The accountant might consider selling accounting software, starting his or her own business, or getting into a completely different career unrelated to managing money. The warehouse worker should apply to facilities where prescription drugs aren't stored.

As always, your interview should emphasize what you can do rather than what you can't. If you had jobs in prison, talk about them just as you would any other job. If you took any vocational courses, stress how that training prepared you for reentry into the workforce. Talk about the tools, machines, and equipment you operated. Bring up the fact that you had to follow orders and work with as diverse a group of people as can be found in any company. Highlight any successes, achievements, or points of pride about the work you've done in prison. In other words, talk about prison work just as if it were done for a Fortune 500 company. You used the same skills—just in a little different work setting.

If you've completed a drug-rehabilitation, anger-management, or any other life-skills course, make sure you point out this achievement to the interviewer.

If you choose your career direction wisely and present a convincing argument that you can do the job well, many employers will, ultimately, overlook previous mistakes. As you prove yourself and gain good work experience, your distant past becomes less and less important.

In preparing yourself for the interview, remember that the interviewer has the right to acquire certain types of information about your convictions, including the following.

- Type of crime committed, how much time was served, and any probation/parole times and limitations

- Severity level of the crime (someone killed, someone injured, property lost, and so on)

- Situation leading to the crime (why did you do it?)

- Rehabilitation efforts undertaken while in jail or prison (got a GED, took anger-management or drug-rehabilitation course, and so on)

- Current situation and what you are doing to continue rehabilitation (continuing in drug/alcohol treatment, taking educational classes, volunteering, and so on)

So, at the very least, an ex-offender needs to be able to supply that information.

Background Checks, Polygraphs, or Other Tests?

Ninety-four percent of employers do some form of background check before hiring someone. Background checks might include checking drug use, credit history, criminal history, education and training, past employer references, and other matters of interest depending on the position. In some cases, an employer will not consider hiring anyone who does not agree to these background checks. Some employers also use computerized or paper tests to identify people who are likely to be dishonest or have other personality-driven job-related problems. You can count on your background being checked if

- The job requires bonding.
- You will have access to money or valuables.
- You will carry a weapon.
- You will drive a company vehicle.
- You will have access to drugs or explosives.
- You will have access to master keys.
- You will have people, children, or patient contact.
- The position requires a check by law.
- The position is a national defense job.
- The position requires confidentiality.

In general, you need to convince an employer that you can be trusted to do a good job. If you have done a good job in preparing your responses, we suggest that you agree to background checks for jobs that interest you. If you have a serious problem in your background, consider in advance how you will handle employer requests to check your background.

Sensitive Questions About Your Personal Situation or Status

Many people consider the issues in this section, including age, race, and gender, inappropriate for an employer to consider when making a decision to hire. Because of this, employers are much more likely to use indirect questions regarding these concerns.

Most employers are wise enough to avoid overtly making decisions based on things that should not matter. Usually, an interviewer hires the candidate who can do the job the best. A good interviewer will allow you to discuss your strengths without lying about them. Your handling of the interview can assure the interviewer that you are not a stereotype. But in order to prevent misconceptions, you must know what these stereotypes might be and address them.

For this reason, even if your "problem" does not come up in the interview, bring it up and deal with it—especially if you think it might really be important to the employer. Don't leave room for ambiguity or doubt when it comes to an issue that might make or break your chances at getting a job you want.

Too Old

Workers over 50 have a harder time finding new jobs in the labor market—and think that older workers are the most discriminated-against group. Not true! The number-one group discriminated against are people in racial minorities such as African Americans and Hispanics. Second are women. Age discrimination comes in a distant third. Many older workers are highly qualified professionals who have lost jobs due to reasons not related to performance. About a third of these displaced workers end up getting higher-paying, better jobs; another third get jobs that pay about the same; and the last third end up worse off.

The reason older workers sometimes do have difficulty finding new jobs is that a number of myths permeate the labor market about older workers. It's your responsibility to counter the negative perceptions associated with each of these myths. The following are some of the more common myths and a couple of ways to counter each of those myths during an interview:

- Older workers can't learn new technology.
  - Talk about times when you've had to adapt to changing technology in previous jobs.
  - Let the interviewer know you're taking computer classes or that you are computer literate.
- Older workers are sick more often.
  - Stress during the interview your attendance record—if it's good.
  - Talk about times when you showed up and younger workers didn't.
- Older workers are more accident-prone.
  - Talk up your safety record or the fact that you've never missed days due to work-related injuries.
  - Highlight safety courses you've taken and ways you have helped develop ideas to improve safety.
- Older workers are slow and nonproductive.
  - Point out that you've recently met production and quality standards in another position.
  - Discuss how your experience helps you do the job right—the first time.
- Older workers aren't flexible.
  - Talk about the times when you've had to do more than just the job you were hired to do.
  - Bring up instances of when you've worked overtime, weekends, or holidays to get the job done.
- Older workers don't interact well with younger workers.
  - Give examples of when you've successfully collaborated with younger workers.
  - Present times when you were supervised by younger workers.

- Older workers cost more.

  - Stress the fact that the employer is buying a level of experience that can't be acquired any other way than by hiring a more mature worker.

  - Indicate that you can bring more to the table regarding decision-making, teamwork, and problem-solving skills than most younger workers.

People with more experience tend to be paid more; but 90 percent of Fortune 400 hiring managers say that they get a better ROI (return on investment) from people with more experience than from younger workers who will probably move on in a few years.

Most employers try to avoid hiring someone who was paid more in his or her previous position. Why? Because they fear that the person earning less than he or she is used to will be unhappy and will leave as soon as a better-paying job becomes available. One of the reasons employers hire a person with less experience is that they assume that such a person will be more satisfied with the pay he or she gets. In addition, many of the new jobs created in the last decade were with smaller companies that just couldn't pay as much as more established firms.

Don't let negative preconceptions about age discourage you. There are some labor market factors working to your advantage—even if it doesn't seem so at times. For starters, understand that there are fewer younger workers now, so employers have no option but to compete for qualified older workers. Retirement is also sapping the knowledge base in many companies. It's estimated that between 25 and 50 percent of skilled workers and managers will be eligible for retirement in the next few years. The hot new HR trend is figuring out how to retain and recruit older workers.

To push the interviewer along that path, present your wealth of experience and maturity as an advantage rather than a disadvantage. Older workers often have some things going for them that younger workers do not. Emphasize your loyalty to previous employers, and highlight accomplishments that occurred over a period of time. If you encounter hesitation after the first interview, meet the fear head-on with a question such as "Are you concerned about compensation?" or "If I could reduce your costs significantly, would you be willing to make me a job offer?"

If you have more than 15 years of work experience, draw upon your more recent work for examples of work habits and successes. Select recent activities that best support your ability to do the job you are now seeking and put the emphasis on them. You don't automatically have to provide details of your work history from earlier times.

Overqualified/Too Much Experience

It doesn't seem like you could have too *much* experience, but some employers think so. They might think you'll become bored and leave, be a "know-it-all" instead of an employee, or feel embarrassed about having a job that is below your previous pay grade or level of responsibility. These are only a few of the fears that wander through interviewers' minds when highly skilled applicants apply for lower-skilled positions.

What an employer needs is some assurance that this is not the case with you. Anytime you get the feeling that the employer is concerned about your "overqualification," you might want to say something like this:

> *You seem to be concerned that I might be overqualified for this position. Are you concerned that I'll leave, that I won't happy, or that I won't fit in with the other workers? Or is it something else?*

If you can find out what's worrying the interviewer, at the very least, you'll have an opportunity to talk it out and put the issue to rest.

A second tactic to consider uses the fact that something rang the interviewer's bell about you or you wouldn't be in the interview. You might want to say something along these lines when the issue of overqualification pops up:

> *There must have been something about me that you liked in my resume, cover letter, or application, or you wouldn't have brought me in for an interview. What was it, and what's worrying you about my background now?*

Employers realize that after a period of unemployment, most people are willing to settle for less. If you are willing to accept a job that you might be defined as overqualified for, be prepared to explain in the interview why you *do* want this particular job and how your wealth of experience is a positive and not a negative. You might also want to assure the interviewer that you plan to stay on the job for at least one or two years as a way to assuage some of his or her fears.

Go out of your way to convince the interviewer that you aren't a job hopper. Maintain high enthusiasm for the organization's future, and present ways you could grow in this position. Suggest how you could assist other departments, solve long-term problems, build profit, and use your experience to help out in other ways.

Too Young

Younger people need to present their youth as an asset rather than a liability. For example, perhaps you are willing to work for less money, accept less-desirable tasks, work longer or less-convenient hours, or do other things that a more experienced worker might not do. If this is true, you should say so in the interview. Emphasize the time and dedication you put into school projects. Above all, conduct yourself with maturity and show some genuine enthusiasm and energy. Let the interviewer know that, even though you have developed some skills in school, you have no bad habits to correct and want to soak up more knowledge.

> **Tip:** Remember that interviewers are also calculating salary requirements during the interview. They don't want to waste their time interviewing someone who will not accept an offer, even though the interviewers might have some flexibility to offer more for the right person. Your task is to not discuss money until the offer is made. See chapter 8 for tips on negotiating pay.

The items in the following worksheet are the results of a study done by Job Search Training Systems, Inc. They asked employers what they wanted from young hires.

Try to think of examples of when you have demonstrated the skills or traits listed here. Make a couple of notes next to each entry so that you don't forget them. The more of these you can talk about in the interview, the better your chances of getting the job.

What Employers Want from Young Workers

Self-confidence   _____

Ability to work independently   _____

Creativity   _____

Professional appearance   _____

(continued)

(continued)

Professional attitude   _____

Positive attitude   _____

Ability to learn   _____

Ambition   _____

Dedication   _____

Interest in the job   _____

Experience or related education   _____

Accuracy   _____

Common sense   _____

Schedule flexibility   _____

Ability to be quick and productive   _____

Loyalty and commitment   _____

Interpersonal skills   _____

Specific job-related skills   _____

Hard worker   _____

Honesty and trustworthiness   _____

Reliability and dependability   _____

Good attendance   _____

If you are turned down in favor of a more experienced worker, don't despair. Keep hammering away at presenting your particular skills, trainability, and available years of dedication. Some employer will be happy to hire you.

New Graduate/Not Enough Experience

Every spring, newspapers across the country blast headlines about how difficult it is for today's graduates to find jobs in their areas of study. Before you start believing the bad press too much, keep in mind that such articles show only one side of the story. Yes, many new grads do find it difficult to find ideal positions with great pay. But this is also true for many more experienced workers.

Remember that small employers are where the action is. Between 2004 and 2005 (the most recent years for which figures are available), companies with fewer than 20 employees added a combined 1.6 million jobs to the nation's work force, according to the report by the SBA's Office of Advocacy. Meanwhile, companies with more than 500 employees lost 181,000 jobs. Smaller organizations are also often more open to letting you take on new projects and directions. This openness allows you to take one job and advance more rapidly to a better one.

Many students recognize that they must take control of their careers and make their own decisions. More than 8 out of 10 students surveyed in the *Right Management Career Expectations and Attitudes Comparison* cited their own interests and skills as the major influence on their career choices. Other traditional influences, including family pressure, anticipated salary, and luck or chance, have dropped significantly in importance. When you interview for a position that matches your personality and talents, your natural enthusiasm for that job goes a long way in impressing interviewers.

If an interviewer ever suggests that as a new graduate you don't have any work experience in the field, you should challenge the statement immediately. The following example shows one way to defend yourself against the assertion that you don't have any experience:

I do have two years of directly related experience that I gained through formal education and training. Going to school paralleled the work setting. I had to use computer software to analyze data. I was required to meet deadlines, demonstrate my team leadership capabilities on projects, interact with culturally diverse groups, and follow the directions of my supervisors—my teachers. I was required to show up daily and complete assignments. I also had to use my organizational and time-management skills, and I put in long hours to get my degree [or certification]. All of these are responsibilities of a manager trainee. As for it not being paid work experience, I paid for that experience in sweat, time, and money. If I'm willing to do this just to prepare for a job in this field, it's a sure bet that I'll do the same thing when I get the job.

Sometimes a good offense is your best defense. Take a look at a number of job descriptions for the position you're seeking and try to find links between the demands of the job and what you did in school.

Another advantage that you don't want to overlook is that many younger people are more comfortable with newer technologies than their elders. This important advantage helps many younger workers gain an edge over their older, but less technology-oriented, competitors. If you fall into the "not enough experience" category, stress any technical expertise you've acquired in school and emphasize the self-management skills you identified in chapter 2 that would tend to overcome a lack of experience.

Tip: *Don't overlook acceptable experiences such as volunteer work, family responsibilities, education, training, or anything else that you might present as legitimate activities in support of your ability to do the work you feel you can do.*

Again, consider expressing a willingness to accept difficult or less-desirable conditions as one way to break into a field and gain experience. For example, indicating that you are willing to work weekends and evenings or are able to travel or relocate might appeal to an employer and open up some possibilities.

If you worked part-time while going to school, make sure you talk about your ability to multitask. Employers like students who have worked to help pay for their educations.

Issues Related to Women

Women have made great progress in many career fields. Many more employers, managers, professionals, and other workers in responsible positions are women than ever before. Even so, some employers and some career areas present barriers to women.

Despite the fact that the number of women in the workforce has increased rapidly, employers still imagine or experience problems with them. The following are some responses to a survey conducted by the Society for Human Resource Management:

- "Working women with children have difficulties finding adequate child care in our area. Time off and absenteeism are big issues for our working mothers."

- "Gaining coworker acceptance of women in nontraditional roles is a serious problem. Many of our executives are uncertain how to manage women."

- "We have more women managers, but few women officers, and none on the board of directors. The glass ceiling is a reality."

Child Care

Men are not likely to be asked about their child care issues prior to being hired and are, according to the Equal Employment Opportunity

Commission, far less likely to experience sexual harassment or gender-related discrimination or prejudice. Interestingly enough, women employers are often just as concerned as male employers are about a woman's family status. Employers of both genders assume that a woman is more likely to have child-related problems. They will want to be certain that these problems do not affect their work.

A *Harvard Business Review* study documented that "on average, working mothers put in an 84-hour work week between their homes and their jobs; working fathers put in 72 hours, and married people with no children put in 50." Those numbers are staggering: A mother essentially holds down two full-time jobs. In addition, caring for elderly parents generally falls on the shoulders of women in our country. For women who have or are likely to have children or elderly parents in need of care, the number-one task is to assure interviewers that they don't intend to abandon their families but do intend to devote the necessary time to the job.

Again, handling questions about child care is simply a matter of turning your situation into a positive. Why not present your resourceful nature by giving an example of how you secured reliable child care? Or illustrate your management skills by describing how you handled work responsibilities when your child was ill and you needed to be at home. Be prepared to back up your loyalty, work ethic, and reliability claims with actual numbers of days missed due to family issues (if the number is low, of course).

Don't make the mistake of assuming that just because a woman interviews you, you don't need to bring up the child-care issue. Even though she might be in the same boat herself, empathy rarely plays a role in landing you a position in a competitive job market. An interviewer's main focus is hiring someone who can do the job—regardless of whether they are a man or a woman.

Status Issues

It seems almost laughable that with the number of women in today's workplace, some interviewers would still be uncertain of how to manage women. However, sensational headlines of sexual harassment and discrimination still abound. According to Carol Price, an educator and lecturer with CareerTrack who specializes in giving power presentations for women, you should begin establishing your equal status the second you walk in the room. "Once you do that, I really believe gender issues go away," she says.

So how do you "establish equal status" without appearing like a militant on a mission—another image of women that frightens employers? Simply look like you belong at the interview. "That means my head is held up, my shoulders are back, I walk in without hesitation, and I put my hand out," says Price. The handshake in particular is crucial. "A handshake was originally devised to prove we were weaponless. In a job interview, that translates to 'you and I are equal in value' when my hand goes out," Price says.

During the interview itself, do not complain about or even mention the lack of opportunity for women at your current or last job as the reason you are seeking new employment. Don't bring up the fact that there might be questions about your competency at all. Assume you are accepted and you will be, Price advises.

Issues Related to Men

Although this topic is seldom discussed, men also face certain biases because of their gender. Men are expected to have steady employment and not take time off for raising a family or caring for older parents. Those who do not aspire to higher status can be quickly branded "losers." You will also find few males in occupations dominated by women such as grade-school teacher, clerical worker, and nurse. Just as with women (but in different ways), men are expected to behave in certain ways, take on certain responsibilities, and quietly accept the limitations imposed on them.

In the recent past, many men have been frustrated with their inabilities to move up in pay and stature. Some big reasons for this are the large number of male baby boomers competing for the limited number of management jobs and the greater number of educated and qualified women in the workforce who want the same things. Higher percentages of women graduate from high school and from college now than men, and some experts predict that this change will result in long-term reductions in earnings of men compared to women. As a result, the competition for jobs has become tough.

Even so, there are not many situations where being a man works against you, particularly if you have a good work history. For example, how many men get questions about their plans to have or care for children or the possibility that they will make a move from the area because their wife takes a more prestigious job in another city? I know that I've never been asked about these issues in past employment interviews.

But let's say that you are a man applying for a job that's stereotypically thought of as a woman's job. It's your challenge to offer proof that you are as qualified and well-suited to the position as the female applicants. Your resume can serve as proof of your related experience. You might also offer up the results of a personality test, such as the Myers-Briggs Type Indicator, showing that your personality is well suited to the position.

Sexual Preference

Sexual preference is an issue for some employers, and unmarried men and women of a certain age might create suspicion as to their sexual preference in some interviewers' minds. Employers' fears are twofold. First, employers do not want their workplaces to become stages for airing social concerns to the detriment of producing products or services. The Society for Human Resource Management reveals that respondents to a survey on these issues said, "We have not encountered any pressures from gay/lesbian groups directly. However, employees continue to voice their concerns about having to work with these groups and the potential risk—real or perceived—that they pose." And "In our traditional, conservative culture, managers have deeply ingrained biases and fears of gay and lesbian employees."

Another concern is economic. Rapidly increasing health-care costs are a serious problem for most organizations. Some employers are concerned about being forced to insure domestic partners because this could substantially increase their health-care costs. And, let's face it, some employers don't want to hire someone with a perceived higher potential for HIV-related costs or simply do not want gay and lesbian people on their staffs.

Although we have advocated directly attacking stereotypes in other categories, we advise gay people to adopt the military's "don't ask, don't tell" policy related to this issue. The risks of divulging such personal information are too great to bring up in an interview, and sexual and domestic matters are not something you should discuss in a job interview, anyway.

Racial or Ethnic Minorities

There always have been, and sadly there always will be, employers who discriminate based on race or ethnicity. The largest minority groups in this country are African American and Hispanic, although there are many smaller groups of recent immigrants, Native Americans, and others. The issue here is discrimination. The good news is that most employers fairly consider hiring a person based on his or her qualifications. Many employers go to great lengths to ensure minority candidates are given fair consideration and to actively recruit minorities. In fact, one of the factors many larger companies use to evaluate candidates is the person's ability to bring some cultural diversity to the company.

The problem is that some employers are less likely to hire a qualified minority based on negative stereotypes. Unfortunately, you are not likely to know which employers are being fair and which are not. Wondering why you are not getting a job offer will drive you nuts, so the best advice is the following:

- Assume that the interviewer is being fair and will consider hiring you based on your skills and abilities.

- In the interview, be yourself and focus on the skills you have to do the job. We give this same advice to everyone because following this procedure is important.

- Consider which stereotypes an employer might harbor and make sure you present details about your situation that would disprove them.

- If the hiring authorities in a company are so biased against minorities, be thankful you won't be working there. Very little good can come from your fighting an uphill battle. We'd advise applying for a job with the major competitor of any company that you find practicing discrimination and openly boycotting the offending company in the future.

If limited proficiency in English is an issue for you, you will need to openly address it. Suggest that you are a good worker and are learning English rapidly, and consider how your multi-language skills would allow you to help the employer provide better service to those who speak your native language.

You might also consider taking a person to translate for you or a handheld translator. Also spend time before the interview translating the career vocabulary of the job from your native language into English and practice using those words during the interview. Needless to say, if the job you're seeking requires high levels of English skills, you're probably interviewing for the wrong job.

Disability-Related Issues

Biases against those with disabilities are common enough that the government passed the Americans with Disabilities Act in 1990 to prevent unfair discrimination. But negative assumptions about people with disabilities are the true barrier you are up against in the interview, no matter how many government agencies exist to back up your eligibility.

According to a Society for Human Resource Management survey, many respondents indicated that accommodating employees with disabilities presents difficulties for their organizations. Here are some specific comments:

- "We are a small organization, and accommodation of physical requirements for disabled workers and time off for illness and medical treatment cause disruption to work and schedules."

- "Some disabled workers are looked upon with disdain by their managers and peers. We have to overcome these attitudes."

I assume you will not seek a job that you can't or should not do. That, of course, would be foolish. So that means you are seeking a job that you are capable of doing, right? That being the case, you don't have a disability related to doing a particular job at all. The employer will still use his or her judgment in hiring the best person for the job, and that means people with disabilities have to compete for jobs along with everyone else. That is fair, so you need to present a convincing argument to employers for why they should hire you over someone else.

It's important to not assume that the person chatting with you understands the technical details of your handicap. I see nothing wrong in casually mentioning how you have worked around your disability in other positions. Just remember to remain matter-of-fact in your explanation. If you avoid a defensive tone at all costs, you will not only put the interviewer at ease, but also assure him or her that your future colleagues will admire your abilities and attitude, too.

There are a couple of other ways to overcome the interviewer's anxiety and their feelings of discomfort in talking to a person with a disability:

- Let interviewers know that they don't have to pussyfoot around the issue of the disability. This shows the interviewers that they won't have to worry too much about how coworkers will react to your being hired and they won't have to worry as much about asking questions that might not be perfectly acceptable under the Americans with Disabilities Act.

- Make a list of objections or fears you think an employer might have about hiring an individual with your specific disability. Next, come up with a way to show the employer that you've already solved the problem or addressed the concern. Here are a couple of examples:

- A person who uses a wheelchair might let the interviewer know they've already found a way to get out of the building in case of a fire.

- A person suffering from vision impairment could let the interviewer know that they already have computer software that translates written words into speech.

> **Tip:** *For more help on overcoming your disability in your job search, see the book* Job Search Handbook for People with Disabilities *by Daniel J. Ryan, Ph.D. (JIST Publishing).*

Don't put the load of finding out about supportive equipment for your disability on the employer. When you walk in the door, you should have information about the types of equipment you might need, where it can be acquired or that you already have it, and what the cost would be.

Some Other Tricky Questions

Most employers avoid asking sensitive questions in a direct way. Instead, they ask indirect questions during the interview in hopes of finding out what they are not "allowed" to ask more directly.

The following questions are all legal, and they give you the opportunity to let an employer know that you and your situation will not be a problem. Think about what might concern an employer regarding your particular situation and plan to cover this during your interview, even if you are not asked about it in a direct way. Your good answer to one of these questions gives you the opportunity to put an employer's real, but perhaps unstated, concern to rest.

- **"What would you like to accomplish during the next 10 [or five] years?"**

  Let the employer know that you have three sets of 10-year goals: educational goals, personal goals, and career-related goals. Outline these for the interviewer. Just make sure your career-related goals are consistent with the needs of the company. Saying you want to learn enough about the field to start your own business shouldn't be an answer to this question.

  Another way to deal with this question is to talk about what you want to achieve on the job, at this company, and for this employer, not for yourself. "I'd like to cut production costs by at least 5 percent and find ways to streamline the layout procedure so that we can add publications without adding staff," is a much better answer than "I'd like to be making 25 percent more in salary and have a corner office."

- **"How long have you been looking for another job?"**

Never give an actual timeframe! Casually reply, "Time isn't a factor because I'm searching for the position that best matches my skills and goals."

- **"What type of person would you hire for this position?"**

Flashback: You're casting your ballot for class president and mark the box for your opponent out of modesty. In doing so, you lost then, and you'll lose now if you don't choose yourself! "I'd hire someone who, beyond a shadow of a doubt, has the skills and people experience to handle this job. I would definitely hire myself."

- **"How do you normally handle criticism?"**

Ah, an easy question if you take it on the chin well. However, most of us aren't that admirable, and we have to put a twist on this common question. The following are a couple of approaches to think about:

"I've heard it said that criticism is a form of flattery. If someone is honestly critiquing my work, they must be interested in helping me do it better."

Or, "Obviously, criticism comes from not doing the job properly, and I'm eager to correct any mistakes or misunderstandings the minute they arise. I'm grateful to the person who cares enough to help me out in that respect."

- **"How do you feel about working overtime and on weekends?"**

If you are willing to work weekends, holidays, or overtime, you'll get a couple of extra interview points. But, if the prospect does not appeal to you, this question can be answered so that your response does not harm you. "I have no problem devoting evening hours and weekends to getting a special project done. I also believe that a balanced life leads to a fresh, energetic employee who is less likely to burn out, so I try to pace myself for a consistent, dependable job performance over the long run, too."

- **"What do you do for fun in your spare time?"**

  This question has a dual motivation behind it. First, the interviewer is confirming your response to the "Will you work overtime?" question. If you replied "yes" to that question, but then outline a lifestyle that involves weekends at a cabin, evenings at the gym, and commitments to various nonprofit and community events, he'll think it's unlikely you'll cancel those plans to work overtime. On the other hand, this is also an opportunity for the interviewer to confirm those things he or she can't legally ask, such as if you have a family, if you attend church, and so on. "My in-laws have a cabin by a nearby lake, and the children enjoy going there on weekends. I accompany them when I can, but sometimes work-related projects prevent that. Of course, the grandparents welcome those times so they can spend one-on-one time with the kids."

- **"Describe your typical day."**

  Naturally, leave out that you aren't a morning person or you start winding down at 4:30 p.m. to hit the parking lot by 5:00 p.m. Use this opportunity to advertise how well you organize yourself and conceptualize long-term projects. "I keep a calendar on my desk with appointment times recorded on the left side and tasks to accomplish that day on the right. I allot time each day to stay in touch with other departments and to return any missed phone calls or e-mail promptly. Overall, my entire day is focused on providing customers with a top-notch product."

- **"What do you like most about your present boss?"**

  For most candidates, finding something nice to say in response to this question is not too hard. Focus your answer on the type of supervision your boss provides and not necessarily on a personality type. "I appreciate the regular feedback" is a more useful response than "I enjoy the fact that he always has an upbeat attitude," even though both are certainly positive answers.

- **"What do you like least about your present boss?"**

  Remember when your folks told you "if you can't say anything good, don't say anything at all"? The concept is sound, but in this instance, you have to say something in order to answer the interviewer's question. One way to walk the razor's edge of this question is to say something like the following:

"I make it a rule to never say anything bad about anyone, especially someone that I have worked with for years and learned so much from."

If pushed for a more specific answer, stick to management principles and skip personality conflicts. You might say

"I would have liked for him to be a better delegator. He had a tendency to take on too much wasn't as able to ask for help as he should have been."

- **"What do you dislike about your previous job?"**

  Watch what you say here. You don't want to get caught saying something negative about a job function you'll have to perform in the new job. Again using the concept of saying nothing if you have nothing good to say, you might want to use this approach:

  "I don't know that there was anything I really disliked about doing the job. There were things I liked doing more than others."

  This turns the answer from a negative to a neutral or a positive. To use this method, however, you have to have a solid grasp of what your daily job duties entailed.

Behavioral Questions

Behavioral questions are in vogue in today's labor market, so it's crucial that you learn how to answer them. The concept behind behavioral questions is simple. Employers believe that your past behavior on the job is a good predictor of your future performance—and research bears this out. That's why reference checking is so valuable to an employer. As we pointed out in an earlier chapter, you can tell it's a behavioral question when the employer asks for an example, a situation, or an instance of when you've used a specific skill.

Behavioral questions are sometime called storytelling questions because your answer to this type of question should come out in a storytelling fashion, where you address the who, what, where, when, why, how, and results in your answer. If you can handle these questions to the interviewer's satisfaction, your chances of getting a job offer go to new highs.

A few of the more common behavioral questions include the following:

Can you give me an example of a time when you…

- …worked effectively under pressure?

- …handled an interpersonal conflict with a coworker?

- …had to show initiative or take a risk solving a problem?

- …motivated others to higher performance?

- …had to manage multiple tasks?

- …were unable to complete a project on time?

- …delegated responsibility effectively?

- …reported on a project to management?

- …anticipated a problem and solved it?

- …made a really difficult decision?

- …were forced to make an unpopular decision?

Many books and job search trainers will tell you to give examples of when you've used your skills successfully. What they often don't tell you is what information should be included in your example. The following sample answer gives you a step-by-step guide to use whenever you're asked for an example, a situation, or a time when you did something.

Notice that the story begins with the name of the company where the example took place and who was reported to. By doing this, you give the interviewer a message that what you're presenting is truthful. Someone trying to hide information, or who tries to make up an example, wouldn't want to give names and places that can be checked out.

Also note the use of quantifiers (numbers) woven into the story and included in the result. The example story is brief, but gives the interviewer all the information he or she needs.

So, if an employer should ever ask you for an example of "when you worked effectively under pressure," or any other question requiring you to give an example, you can follow this basic five-step pattern and improve your interview impact:

1. **Where were you working and what was your role?** "When I was working for Smith Builders as the construction foreman…"

2. **Who did you report to?** "…the boss, Fred Lyle, told me that…"

3. **What was the problem to solve or what situation were you in?** "…my building crew had to completely frame a tri-level home in one day, when it normally takes two days, or the company would lose a $174,000 home sale—even though I was short a man due to illness."

4. **What actions did you take to solve the problem?** "I pulled everyone in the crew together, told them the situation, and asked for some ideas on how we could get the job done on time. I got the crew to agree to split the missing crew member's job between them and to come in early and work late. I found ways to save lots of time by rigging the saw so that we could cut 12 studs at once, and I leased some equipment to set the trusses on the top plate instead of humping them by hand."

5. **What was the result of your actions?** "The job got done on time with no loss of quality, my boss was happy, the company made $174,000, and I took my crew out to dinner for their extra effort."

Interview Techniques Employers Use to Psych You Out

Employers today are all too aware of the costs associated with hiring the wrong person. Those costs can range from 5 percent to 150 percent of an employee's gross wages. So employers want to be sure they hire the best candidate. That desire can lead them into trying to "trick" you into admitting background weaknesses, questionable ethics, and personal secrets that indicate you cannot handle the job. Although some interview techniques appear quite innocent, their effects can be deadly if you are unaware of what is happening.

Keep in mind, though, that turnabout is fair play. You can prepare for these devious interviewers by knowing what to do when subjected to scrutiny. As always, I am not encouraging you to lie but to know in advance that your task in an interview is to emphasize your strengths, not reveal your weaknesses. If you have been honest in assessing your skills and have targeted a job that you feel confident about, you need only tell the truth and leave out all irrelevant information.

Although most interviewers will know less about interviewing than you (because you have read this book), some will be masters of the craft. Books have also been written to help professional interviewers, and one of my all-time favorites is *The Evaluation Interview*. Written by Richard Fear, this book is a must-read for interviewers wanting to increase their ability to manipulate an unsuspecting job seeker. Following are some of Fear's suggested techniques for eliciting negative information. Learn to recognize them so they cannot be used to eliminate you from consideration.

- **Misleading facial expressions:** Just as you use your body language—leaning forward, smiling, making good eye contact—to express interest, the interviewer might also attempt to guide your answers with physical cues such as facial expressions. For instance, lifting the eyebrows a little and smiling slightly conveys that the listener is receptive and expectant—and that is all it takes to convince some people to divulge negative facts about themselves to their new "friend." This half-smile and raised eyebrows routine also takes the edge off a delicate or personal question. Don't be misled: You must still answer these sensitive questions with the careful wording you have rehearsed, no matter how interested and nonjudgmental the interviewer appears.

- **Calculated pauses:** Experienced journalists have long elicited information from hard-boiled criminals, slick-tongued politicians, and interview-savvy celebrities by using the calculated pause. The technique works even better on job applicants. Most of us are not comfortable with silence and rush to fill the void with verbal noise. Therefore, when the interviewer says nothing but maintains eye contact, most job seekers feel pressured into either giving more details to their answers or starting another topic altogether.

The best way to handle silence is by remaining quiet and appearing pleasant. This response creates a nonhostile standoff, and in the interest of time, the interviewer eventually asks the next question. Most pauses are measured in seconds, and it is rare for more than two to pass without the interviewer realizing you have not fallen for this ploy. If you are compelled to say something, at least turn the tables. "I think that answers the question, unless there is something else you wish to know," forces the interviewer to become the respondent.

Red-Flag Words and Phrases

Here, according to Richard Fear, are the most common words or phrases an experienced interviewer will use to encourage you to give negative information:

- To what extent did you…?
- How do you feel about/like…?

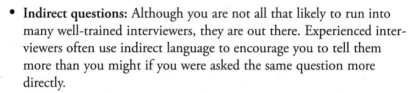

- Is it possible that...?
- How did you happen to...?
- Has there been any opportunity to...?
- To what do you attribute...?
- Might...
- Perhaps...
- Somewhat...
- A little bit...

- **Indirect questions:** Although you are not all that likely to run into many well-trained interviewers, they are out there. Experienced interviewers often use indirect language to encourage you to tell them more than you might if you were asked the same question more directly.

  During the course of an interview, keep your ears tuned for phrases such as "To what extent did you...?" "How did you feel about/like...?" and "Is it possible that...?" Fear calls these phrases "wonderful" and "remarkably effective" because they turn leading questions into open-ended ones. But don't be lulled into missing their sting: "To what extent were you successful on that job?" still carries the meaning of its harsher counterpart, "Were you successful on that job?" Keep your answers directed toward satisfying the more direct question, and your value will jump in the interviewer's estimation.

- **Two-step interview questions:** Just as a dance partner leads you through a series of premeditated steps to complete a specific dance, the interviewer uses questions that are designed to guide you into an overall pattern. The best way for an interviewer to do this is to introduce a general subject and then hone in on the reason for your answer. The method works like this: The interviewer leads off a round of questions with a query such as "What subject did you decide to major in?" He or she then comes back with "Why?"

  Interviewers use the two-step method to probe for clues revealing your judgment, your motivation, and other factors of your personality. So do not think you are completely off the hook with a smooth answer like "History, because I believe it ultimately holds the solutions to problems in the future." When you are in the hands of a master interviewer, he or she is likely to ask you why that aspect seems important to you or why that compelled you to spend four years devoted to it instead of just taking a course or two. The best way to perform the two-step is to be prepared before you ever enter the interviewer's office. The more you understand yourself, the more gracefully the two of you will dance.

- **Laundry-list questions:** Beware of questions that offer a variety of options from which to choose (the so-called laundry list). The interviewer is not always trying to help you think in a stressful situation. In fact, it is just the opposite. When interviewers throw out a question with a series of possibilities from which to select, they are often trying to confirm details they picked up from a previous comment you made. Richard Fear provides an example: Assume that you, the applicant, have dropped some hints that seem to indicate a dislike for detail. The interviewer can often follow up on such clues by including a reference to detail in the laundry-list question at the end of the discussion of work history.

- **Forced-choice questions:** Another tricky technique interviewers use to probe job seekers' weaknesses is the forced-choice question. It is called this because you are asked to choose between a rock and a hard place: You won't choose the first option presented unless you have a high degree of skill or personality in that area; the second option is phrased so that it is easy to choose it, even though it is the less desirable one. Ouch!

  Here is an example: "What about your spelling ability—do you have that ability to the extent that you would like, or is that something you could improve a little bit?" (Notice the liberal use of softening words thrown in for good measure.) If you select the first option, it implies you feel no need for improvement—and you had better be prepared to back that up with perfect spelling! The second choice invites you to confess you are not up to speed in this area.

  Your best answer to a double-edged question is to frame it in the context of your strengths. Here's a sample response: "Because I'm a perfectionist, my spelling ability probably will not ever be what I hope for, but I am an above-average speller. And I am very careful to check any words that I am not sure of so that no spelling errors remain."

Key Points: Chapter 5

- Think about the things in your background that an employer might interpret as negative. Then make sure you have a response ready that will help turn those negatives into positives.

- Make a list of questions that will be difficult for you to answer. Review the list of questions at the end of chapter 4 and include any you find there that you need to work on.

- Use the Three-Step Process to answering interview questions in chapter 4 to present your situation honestly and positively.

- Ask someone you know to ask you these difficult questions and practice answering them.

Chapter 6

How to Close the Interview and Leave a Lasting Impression

L et's say you're nearing the end of the interview and have answered all of the interviewer's questions to the best of your ability. At this point (usually about 55 minutes or less for nonexempt workers and somewhere around 80 to 90 minutes for management or supervisory positions) the interviewer will stand up and say something like this, "Thank you for coming in, we'll get back with you when we make a decision." It's at this point that most applicants make a critical mistake. They just say thank you, shake the interviewer's hand, and walk out of the interview.

Interviewees who walk away lose a great opportunity to create a lasting and positive final impression on the interviewer. They also leave without information on the next step or where they rank against other applicants.

Remember this about interviewers: Interviewers have a tendency to remember very strongly what they see and hear early on during an interview. That's why it's so important to create a good first impression. But interviewers also remember very strongly what they see and hear at the end of the interview. So how you leave the interview is one of the most crucial points in your whole job search process.

Six Goals for the End of the Interview

There are six goals you want to achieve at the end of the interview to maximize your impact and set you apart from the competition:

1. You want to do something unique so that the interviewer will remember your face and set you apart from the competition.

2. You want to let the interviewer know you want the job. Less than 10 percent of applicants ever do this.

3. You want to make a personal commitment to the interviewer as a way to assuage his or her fear of making a bad hire.

4. You want to try to schedule a time to "personally" follow up by phone—for a number of reasons. Why?

   - More than 80 percent of employers complain about a lack of appropriate follow-up after an interview.

   - You can ask questions you thought about after you left the interview.

   - It will keep you fresh in the interviewer's mind.

5. You want to try to find out where you stand and if there are any concerns the interviewer might have about you.

6. You want to find out the next step in the hiring process and the time frames for a decision.

Methods for Making a Big Final Impression

The following sections present two of the best ways to make a lasting impression.

The Call-Back Close

One of the best ways to close an interview is with an old sales technique that's called the Call-Back Close. This approach requires some courage, some practice, and a little thinking on your feet, but it works.

Here's how it works:

1. **Thank the interviewer by name and let him or her know you appreciate his or her time.** While shaking hands, say, "Thank you, Mr. [or Mrs. or Ms.] _____ for your time today. I know how time-consuming and difficult this process must be for you."

2. **Let them know you want the job.** Depending on the situation, express your interest in the job, organization, service, or product by saying, "I'm very interested in the ideas we went over today," or "I'm very interested in your organization. It seems to be an exciting place to work." Or confidently say, "I am definitely interested in this position."

3. **Link your skills to the job and make a personal commitment.** "It seems like my skills and personality fit pretty well, and I promise you that I'll be a valuable employee and will work hard to live up to your expectations."

4. **Mention your busy schedule and arrange a reason and a time to call back.** "Because I'm in job search mode, I'll be networking, researching, and out of the house quite a bit. What I'd like to do is get a date and time when I can call you back, because I'm sure I'll have questions after I think about the interview a little more. When is the best time for me to get back with you? End of next week or beginning? Morning or afternoon?" Notice that I said "when" rather than "is it okay to…" because asking when does not easily allow a "no" response. A forced-response question is also used to get a specific day and a best time to call. And, if you have a preferred time, remember to list it last while presenting options to the interviewer. People generally answer with whatever option you give last.

5. **Check for problems and your ranking against the competition.** "Before leaving, can you tell me how I stack up against the competition and if there are any concerns you might have that I didn't address in the interview?"

6. **Find out the next step.** "Can you also tell me what's the next step and when you plan on making a hiring decision?"

7. **Give them a JIST Card** (see the next section). As you begin to leave, say something like, "Here's a summary of my skills. I don't want you to forget me." And then hand them your card.

8. **Pay attention to the assistant.** As you leave, thank the assistant by name, tell her you hope you get the job, and give her a JIST Card. You might say something like this, "Thanks a lot, Mrs. Oliver. I hope I get the opportunity to work here. Here's a summary of my skills for easy reference should anyone here need it."

The JIST Card®: A Mini Resume and a Powerful Job Search Tool

A big bang can come in a little package. A team of America's best job search trainers developed the JIST Card to help job seekers. The trainers found that it is beneficial as a networking tool. It can also provide the foundation for a more confident interview answer to the question, "Can you tell me about yourself?" Giving a JIST Card to an interviewer as you leave the interview is a great way to leave a lasting and positive impression.

JIST Cards are carefully constructed to contain all the essential information most employers want to know in a very short format. In its simplest form, the JIST Card typically uses a 3 × 5–inch card format, but the size has evolved over time. Figure 6.1 shows a basic design for you to consider.

(front)

Willie B. Nice

Position Desired
Customer Service Representative

Phone: 317-123-4567
Pager: 317-123-4568
Cell: 317-123-4569
E-mail: goodworker@email.com

(back)

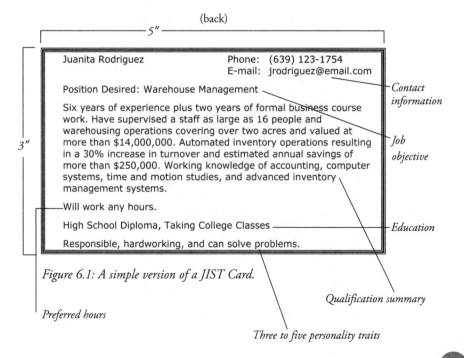

├─────── *5"* ───────┤

Juanita Rodriguez   Phone: (639) 123-1754
                           E-mail: jrodriguez@email.com

Position Desired: Warehouse Management ⟶ *Contact information*

Six years of experience plus two years of formal business course work. Have supervised a staff as large as 16 people and warehousing operations covering over two acres and valued at more than $14,000,000. Automated inventory operations resulting in a 30% increase in turnover and estimated annual savings of more than $250,000. Working knowledge of accounting, computer systems, time and motion studies, and advanced inventory management systems. — *Job objective*

Will work any hours.

High School Diploma, Taking College Classes ─── *Education*

Responsible, hardworking, and can solve problems.

3"

Figure 6.1: A simple version of a JIST Card.

Qualification summary

Preferred hours

Three to five personality traits

In figure 6.2, you can see how a more advanced style JIST Card can be turned into a bi-fold card. You can change the size or add and remove different types of information. You can be as creative as you want with how you arrange the information.

Caution: *Unless the job you want is graphic or artistic in nature, keep the card as simple as possible. Remember, it's a business card, not artwork.*

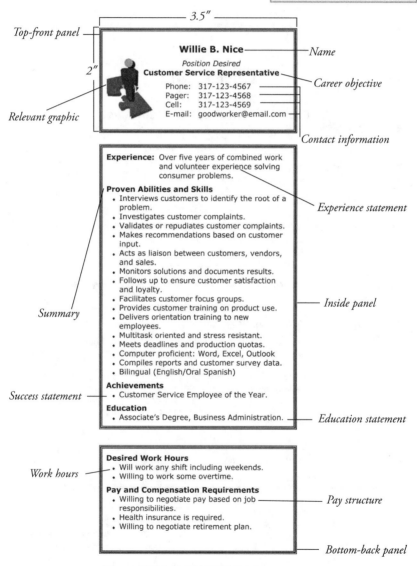

Figure 6.2: A bi-fold JIST Card.

Why the JIST Card Works

In reality, a job seeker is a product that needs to be marketed. One of the most common ways for people in the business world to market their products or services is by handing out business cards (not resumes) to let prospective customers know who they are, what they can offer, and how to contact them. A well-designed JIST Card will act as your business card while you're looking for work.

Here are some reasons why using a JIST Card can help you find a job faster:

- A JIST Card is more akin to a business-marketing tool than a resume.

- It's unusual, concise, graphic, and memorable.

- It's to-the-point and shows how you will meet the employer's needs.

- It's a physical reminder of who you are and what you can do when it's given at the end of the interview.

Using JIST Cards

Usage is the place to be creative with your JIST Card. Following are some of the ways you can use them:

- Include them in thank-you notes.

- Use them as a networking tool. Everyone you know or meet should get a couple. Ask people if they'll give them to one of their contacts.

- Give one to the interviewer at the end of an interview.

- Give them to the administrative assistant at your interview.

However you decide to use them, remember that 90 percent of employers say these cards make a favorable impression.

Key Points: Chapter 6

- Your goals for the end of the interview are to be memorable, let the interviewer know you want the job, make a personal commitment to the employer, schedule your follow-up call, answer any concerns, and find out the next steps and time frame.

- The two best ways to make a big impression at the end of the interview is to use the Call-Back Close method and leave a copy of your JIST Card with the employer.

Chapter 7

Following Up After the Interview

It's tomorrow night and your interview has ended. You made it home. Now it's all over, right? Wrong. Effective follow-up actions can make a big difference in whether you get a job offer.

What to Do as Soon as You Get Home

Following up can make the difference between being unemployed or underemployed and getting the job you want fast. When you get home from the interview tomorrow, do the following:

- **Make notes on the interview.** While it's fresh in your mind, jot down key points. A week later, you might not remember something essential.

- **Schedule your follow-up.** If you agreed to call back next Monday between 9:00 a.m. and 10:00 a.m., you are likely to forget unless you put it on your schedule.

- **Send your thank-you note.** Send thank-you notes the very same day if possible. Send an e-mail thank-you that day, and then follow this with a thank-you note through regular mail.

- **Call when you said you would!** Calling when you say you will creates the impression of organization and a desire for the job. If you do have a specific question, ask it at this time. If you want the job, say that you want it and explain why. If the position has been filled, say you enjoyed the visit and would like to continue to stay in touch during your job search. If you were referred to others, let the interviewer know how these contacts went. Ask the interviewer what he or she suggests your next step should be. This would also be a good time to ask, if you have not done so before, for the names of anyone else with whom you might speak about a position for a person with your skills and experience.

- **Schedule more follow-up.** Set a time to talk with this person again. And, of course, send the interviewer another thank-you note or e-mail.

The rest of this chapter details several ways to follow up with employers after the interview.

The Importance of Thank-You Notes

Resumes and cover letters get the attention, but thank-you notes often get results. Wouldn't you like to receive a letter or call saying, "Thank you for taking the time to interview with us. We've selected you to fill the position"? Sending thank-you notes shows good manners and makes good job search sense for a couple of reasons:

- A survey done by Job Search Training Systems, Inc., found that more than 80 percent of employers felt a thank-you note was beneficial as a way to follow up after the interview and had a positive impact on the hiring decision. Other research results also support this.

- A thank-you note gives you the rare chance to change a first impression. If there is anything from the interview that you think might be of concern to the interviewer, a thank-you note allows you to address it and correct any misconceptions.

Three Times When You Should Definitely Send Thank-You Notes—and Why

Thank-you notes have a more intimate and friendly social tradition than formal and manipulative business correspondence. I think that is one reason they work so well—people respond to those who show good manners and say thank you. Here are some situations when you should use them, along with some sample notes.

Before an Interview

You can send a less formal note before an interview by e-mail. Simply thank the interviewer for being willing to see you. Attaching a resume to the message would be inappropriate. Remember, this note is supposed to be a sincere thanks for help and not an assertive business correspondence. This note also serves as a gentle reminder to the recipient that you will be showing up tomorrow.

After an Interview

One of the best times to send a thank-you note is right after an interview. The following are several reasons why:

- Doing so creates a positive impression. The employer will assume you have good follow-up skills as well as good manners.

- It creates yet another opportunity for you to be in the employer's thoughts at an important time.

- It gives you a chance to get in the last-word. You get to include a subtle reminder of why you're the best candidate for the job and can address any concerns that might have come up during the interview.

- If the employer has buried, passed along, or otherwise lost your resume and previous correspondence, a thank-you note and enclosed JIST Card provide one more chance for that person to see your number and call you.

For these reasons, we suggest you send a thank-you note right after the interview (within 24 hours). Figure 7.1 is an example of a good thank-you note.

August 11, 20XX

Dear Mr. O'Beel,

Thank you for the opportunity to interview for the position available in your production department. I want you to know that this is the sort of job I have been looking for, and I am enthusiastic about the possibility of working for you.

Now that we have spoken, I know that I have both the experience and skills to fit nicely into your organization and to be productive quickly. The process improvements I implemented at Logistics, Inc., increased their productivity 34%, and I'm confident that I could do the same for you.

Thanks again for the interview; I enjoyed the visit.

Sara Smith

(505) 665-0090

Figure 7.1: A sample post-interview thank-you note.

Whenever Anyone Helps You in Your Job Search

Send a thank-you note to anyone who helps you during your job search. This includes those who give you referrals, people who provide advice, and those who offer support during your search. Figure 7.2 shows an example of this type of note.

> **Tip:** *Send a thank-you note by both e-mail and then regular mail as soon as possible after an interview or meeting. This time is when you are freshest in the mind of the person who receives it and are most likely to make a good impression.*

October 31, 20XX
2234 Riverbed Ave.
Philadelphia, PA 17963

Ms. Helen A. Colcord
Henderson and Associates, Inc.
1801 Washington Blvd., Suite 1201
Philadelphia, PA 17963

Dear Ms. Colcord,

Thank you for sharing your time with me so generously yesterday. I really appreciated talking to you about your career field.

The information you shared with me increased my desire to work in such an area. Your advice has already proven helpful—I have an appointment to meet with Robert Hopper on Friday.

In case you think of someone else who might need a person like me, I'm enclosing another resume and JIST Card.

Sincerely,

Debbie Childs

Figure 7.2: A sample thank-you note to someone who helps you in your job search.

Seven Quick Tips for Writing Thank-You Notes

Use these tips to help you write your thank-you notes.

1. Use Both E-mail and Regular Mail

Consider the timing involved. If you know the employer will be making a decision soon, e-mail is your best bet. But there's something to be said for actually receiving a piece of real mail, opening it, and reading it (as long as it's not a bill). Regular mail makes things a bit more personal. The other person will appreciate the formality of a business letter printed on nice paper and received in the mail.

2. Use Quality Paper and Envelopes

Use good quality notepaper with matching envelopes. Most stationery stores offer thank-you note cards and envelopes in a variety of styles. Select a note that is simple and professional—avoid cute graphics and sayings. A blank card or simple "Thank You" on the front will do. For a professional look, match your resume and notepaper by getting them at the same time. We suggest off-white or buff colors.

3. Decide Whether Handwritten or Computer Printed Is Best

At one time, thank-you notes were handwritten, but most are computer generated and printed these days. If your handwriting is good, writing them is perfectly acceptable and can be a nice touch. If not, type it.

4. Use a Formal Salutation

Don't use a first name unless you've already met the person you're writing to and he or she has asked you to use first names, or you're writing to someone in a young, hip environment. Instead, use "Dear Ms. Smith" or "Ms. Smith," rather than the less formal "Dear Pam." Include the date.

5. Keep the Note Informal and Friendly

Keep your note short and friendly. Remember, the note is a thank-you for what someone else did, not a hard-sell pitch for what you want. Make sure, though, to give a subtle, gentle reminder of your skills or other job-related qualifications. This reminder lets your thank-you note serve as not only an expression of appreciation but also as a chance to get the last word on why you should be hired. The more savvy members of your competition will be including this, so you had better include it, too.

Also, make sure your thank-you note does not sound like a form letter. Put some time and effort into it to tailor it to the recipient and the situation. As appropriate, be specific about when you will next contact the person. If you plan to meet soon, still send a note saying that you look forward to the meeting and say thank-you for the appointment. And make sure that you include something—such as a JIST Card—to remind the employer of who you are and how to reach you, because your name alone might not be enough to be remembered.

6. Sign It

Sign your first and last names. Avoid initials and make your signature legible (unless you're being hired for your creative talents, in which case a wacky-looking, illegible signature could be a plus!).

7. Send It Right Away

Write and send your note no later than 24 hours after you make your contact. Ideally, you should write it immediately after the contact while the details are fresh in your and the interviewer's minds.

> **Tip:** _Always send a note and e-mail after an interview, even if things did not go well. It can't hurt (unless, of course, it's full of typos)._

8. Make Sure Your Contact Information Is Accurate

Misspelling names, not including the person's title, miswriting the address, and listing the wrong department are sure ways to honk off the interviewer and show him or her that you lack attention to detail.

9. Multiple Interviewers = Multiple Thank-You Notes

If more than one person has interviewed you, each person should receive a thank-you note. But don't clone the note for everyone. Each note should be unique. Make sure you mention something each of them asked or did, or how each made an impression on you. You can count on them comparing the notes you sent to see whether it's just a form note.

10. Humanize Your Thank-You Note

Write like you talk and be who you are. Don't mimic a sample or use template notes that sound like they came out of the cookie cutter. Let your personality shine through. If the interviewer doesn't like you for who you are, you probably wouldn't like working with him or her, anyway.

More Sample Thank-You Notes

The following are a few more samples of thank-you notes and letters. They cover a variety of situations and provide ideas on how to structure your own correspondence. Notice that they are all short and friendly and typically mention that the writer will follow up in the future—a key element of a successful job search campaign.

Also note that several of these candidates are following up on interviews where no specific job opening exists yet. For future reference, remember that getting interviews before a job opening exists is a very smart thing to do. All of these examples came from David Swanson's book titled *The Resume Solution* (with minor adjustments to include fictitious e-mail addresses) and are used with permission.

April 22, 20XX

Dear Mr. Nelson,

Thank you so much for seeing me while I was in town last week. I am grateful for your kindness, the interview, and all the information you gave me.

I will call you once again in a few weeks to see if any openings have developed in your marketing research department's planned expansion.

Appreciatively,

Phil Simons

Voice mail: (633) 299-3034

E-mail: psimons@email.com

Figure 7.3: A thank-you note for an informational meeting.

September 17, 20XX

Mr. Bill Kenner
Sales Manager
WRTV
Rochester, MN 87236

Dear Mr. Kenner:

Thank you very much for the interview and the market information you gave me yesterday. I was most impressed with the city, your station, and with everyone I met.

As you requested, I am enclosing a resume and have requested that my former manager call you on Tuesday, the 27th, at 10 a.m.

Working at WRTV with you and your team would be both interesting and exciting for me. I look forward to your reply and the possibility of helping you set new records next year.

Sincerely,

Anne Bently
1434 River Dr.
Polo, WA 99656
Pager: (545) 555-0032

Figure 7.4: A thank-you note after an interview.

October 14, 20XX

Dear Bill,

I really appreciate your recommending me to Alan Stevens at Wexler Cadillac. We met yesterday for almost an hour, and we're having lunch again on Friday. If this develops into a job offer, as you think it may, I will be most grateful.

Enclosed is a reference letter by my summer employer. I thought you might find this helpful.

You're a good friend, and I appreciate your thinking of me.

Sincerely,

Dave

Figure 7.5: A thank-you note to someone who helped you in your search.

July 26, 20XX

Dear Ms. Bailey,

Thank you for the interview for the auditor's job last week.

I appreciate the information you gave me and the opportunity to interview with John Petero. He asked me for a transcript, which I am forwarding today.

Working in my field of finance in a respected firm such as Barry Productions appeals to me greatly. I appreciate your consideration and look forward to hearing from you.

Sincerely,

Dan Rehling
Cell phone: 404-991-3443

Figure 7.6: A thank-you note after an interview with additional information enclosed.

May 21, 20XX

Mrs. Sandra Waller
Yellow Side Stores
778 Northwest Blvd.
Seattle, WA 99659

Dear Ms. Waller:

Thank you so much for the interview you gave me last Friday for the Retail Management Training Program. I learned a great deal and know now that retailing is my first choice for a career.

I look forward to interviewing with Mr. Daniel and Ms. Sobczak next week. For that meeting, I will bring two copies of my resume and a transcript, as you suggested.

Enclosed is a copy of a reference letter written by my summer employer. I thought you might find it helpful.

Sincerely,

Elizabeth Duncan

Figure 7.7: A thank-you note after a first interview and before a second interview.

A Thank-You Note on Steroids

Another type of thank-you note is one that does more than just thank the interviewer and gently nudge him or her to hire you. A thank-you note on steroids includes something extra, such as

- A research article about the field

- A newspaper clipping about the company's product or services

- Something you found out from one of the company's competitors

- Information from the Chamber of Commerce

- Insights you found out about by talking with employees of the company

Figure 7.8 is a sample.

Good Day Mr. Bigbossman,

I just wanted to thank you for investing your valuable time in letting me know about your company and for interviewing me to see how my rubber manufacturing and production experience can meet some of your needs. I'm really excited about the opportunity to work for Rubber Bozos Inc.

After leaving the interview, I wanted to learn more about the technology you use to bond plastic, so I did a little research. Here's an article I found in Rubber Manufacturing News about a new method of bonding rubber products using microwaves instead of chemicals. We didn't talk about this method during our interview, and I thought you might like to see the article.

Sincerely,

Job E. Seeker

Figure 7.8: A sample thank-you note on steroids.

Follow-Up Letters

After an interview, you might want to send some follow-up correspondence in order to solve a problem or present a proposal. We have already shown you some examples of thank-you letters and notes that were sent following an interview. In some cases, a longer or more detailed letter is appropriate. This type of letter provides additional information or presents a proposal.

If there is already a job opening available, you could submit an outline of what you would do if hired. If no job is available, you could submit a proposal that would create a job and state what you would do to make hiring you pay off.

Sending Formal Letters via E-mail

Many hiring managers prefer getting correspondence via e-mail. It's easy, free, and instantaneous. If the employer gives you his or her card with an e-mail address, corresponding via e-mail is generally acceptable. However, if you have a formal cover letter or thank-you note template and send these as e-mail attachments, make sure they are in a universal format such as Microsoft Word or Adobe PDF. Always mention the format of your letter in your e-mail message. If you are ever in doubt about whether an employer can open your attachments, you should directly type (or copy and paste) the cover letter or thank-you note into the body of your e-mail.

In writing such a proposal, you must be specific in telling the hiring manager what you would do and what results your actions would bring. For example, if you proposed you could increase sales, how would you do it and how much might profits increase? Tell employers what you could accomplish and they might just create a new position for you. It happens more often than you probably realize.

Whatever the situation, your post-interview letter should deal with any concerns the employer might have had with you during the interview in a positive way. For example, if the employer voiced concern over a lack of specific experience, you would address his or her concern by stating that you are a quick study, self-motivated, and detail-oriented. Once you have put the employer's concerns to rest, reinforce your interest in the job. Include a statement like, "After hearing more about the job, I am even more certain my skills and education will be beneficial to your company. I am eager to begin working for you and will call next Tuesday to inquire about the hiring decision."

Follow-Up Phone Calls

You probably know of someone who just kept calling or going back to an employer, even if there wasn't an immediate opening, and he or she ended up with a job offer. This is called a "persistence hire." A lot of job seekers think they just wore the employer down. Nothing could be further from the truth. What the person did is show the employer some "sticktuitiveness." He or she stayed on the employer's radar until there was an opportunity to bring him or her on board. Always remember that the labor market is in a perpetual state of flux and job opportunities are created daily by

- A need for weekend, holiday, or vacation coverage.

- A need for new workers because of expansion.

- A need to fill a position because of termination, pregnancy, someone quitting, someone relocating, someone being promoted, and so on.

It's cheaper and easier for the company to hire someone who shows interest in the company—and is already a known commodity—than it is for the company to find someone through traditional recruitment methods.

Although you don't want to become a pest, many employers are favorably impressed with job seekers who follow up by phone. Most job seekers are not nearly as aggressive as they should be in staying in touch with employers after interviews.

Use the following tips to improve your results when following up with phone calls:

- **Ask when would be a good time to call.** Before you leave the interview, ask when would be a good time to call back and note that time on your schedule.

- **Ask about the acceptable frequency of call backs.** The first time you make a call, ask how often you should call back (once a week, every month, every quarter, and so on). This way you can ensure you're not being a pain in the butt.

- **Phone when you said you would.** Call back on the day and at the time the interviewer suggested. By then, if you have done as I suggested, he or she will have received your thank-you e-mail and note. This will likely create a good impression, as will your calling back.

- **If there is an opening, ask for it.** If you want the job, say so. Tell the interviewer why you want it and why you think it is a good fit for you.

- **Be brave; call back on a regular basis.** If the employers you are meeting with don't have an opening for you now, ask to stay in touch. Make it clear that you are interested in working for them and would like to call or e-mail them back on a regular basis to see how things are developing. This kind of contact will keep you in their minds. As positions come up that fit your skills, these employers are more likely to consider you before they advertise the job. But this will happen *only* if you stay in contact with them on a regular basis!

- **Ask for referrals.** Each time you contact employers, ask whether they know of anyone else who might have a job opening for someone with your skills. If not, ask whether they can give you names of others to contact to see whether they have openings.

Key Points: Chapter 7

- After an interview, immediately write your thank-you notes.

- Thank-you notes are a friendly and effective way to demonstrate your good manners and create a positive impression in the minds of employers.

- In some situations, you might want to send a follow-up letter to provide the employer with more information, present a proposal, or clear up any issues that came up in the interview.

- Staying in touch with an employer by phone can be a good way to ask for the job you want, find out about future opportunities, and get referrals to other potential employers.

Chapter 8

Negotiating Your Salary

The salary negotiation is the most important three minutes of an interview and your salary is probably the reason you're looking for work in the first place. Even so, few job seekers are prepared to discuss their pay requirements prior to a job offer or to negotiate it well after a job offer is made. As a result of their blunders, many job seekers are eliminated from consideration during the selection process without even knowing why. Others who do get job offers too often mishandle discussions of pay, resulting in their being paid less than they might have—or losing a job offer completely. In today's economy, passive acceptance can cost us more than we can afford to lose.

A higher starting salary is also a gift that keeps on giving, because all future raises are tied to that starting salary. A little arithmetic might be in order here:

1. An 18-year-old high school graduate negotiates for $21,000 per year instead of accepting the $20,000 per year that was initially offered.

2. That graduate then gets an average 3 percent raise each year.

3. He or she works for 50 years (normal in today's world).

4. The result is that this person ends up with at least $112,000 more during the course of his or her career lifetime than a person who didn't negotiate for that extra $1,000.

Even though there's money to be made by negotiating, the fact is that most people don't negotiate their salaries at all. There are three simple reasons why this happens:

- Few job seekers know how to negotiate effectively. Because of this, they fall prey to a number of salary negotiation mistakes.

- Most job seekers erroneously believe that employers aren't willing to negotiate.

- People are afraid of losing a job offer if they don't immediately accept what is being offered.

The reasons individuals give for not preparing for salary negotiations, such as, "I didn't realize the subject would come up so quickly and didn't have time to prepare" or, "I could tell the interviewer wasn't going to budge, and I didn't want to blow the opportunity," can often be boiled down to one excuse: Most of us are uncomfortable putting a dollar value on our skills.

"The reason many of us are hesitant to take our foot off the brake, get off our butts, and let people know who we are and what we do well is because we feel it is tasteless and unprofessional to do so," says behavioral scientist George Dudley. "We reached that conclusion because the people who have done it in the past are so oily. 'If I have to be like them to do that,' the logic runs, 'then I don't want to do it.'" Michael Schatzki of Negotiation Dynamics has an even more colorful way of describing job seekers' lack of enthusiasm for salary negotiations. "They see it as high stakes, table-pounding, your worst nightmare of a used-car salesman, and it all seems negative," he comments.

In the business world, modesty will get you nowhere. There is nothing shameful about asking for the amount of money you are worth. In today's environment, knowing yourself and your capabilities is a valuable commodity in itself.

Salary Negotiation Mistakes

To negotiate a higher starting pay and a more satisfying job, you first need to understand some of the most common salary negotiation mistakes untrained job seekers make:

1. **Thinking pay and benefits aren't negotiable:** More than 80 percent of employers expect some form of negotiation for pay, benefits, perks, work schedules, work locations, and so on. If you don't ask for it, you won't get it.

2. **Giving up too quickly:** Just because you're told no, doesn't mean the negotiations are over. Salespeople know that the first no is just the start of the sale. Keep plugging away. Patience and persistence are the paths to success.

3. **Saying yes too quickly:** Most of the time the first offer isn't the last offer. And the first offer will usually be lower than the last offer. One theme running through every book on salary negotiation is that interviewees need to delay talking about salary expectations. The longer that an interviewer talks to you, the more likely you'll be to negotiate better compensation.

4. **Not knowing your worth:** Local labor market research is your friend. Don't put off doing it. Undervaluing and overvaluing your skills are interview bear traps. Walking into an interview not knowing what the high, low, and average salary and compensation levels are for a person with your skills, experience, and education is like gambling in Vegas without knowing the rules: You always lose.

5. **Negotiating at the wrong time:** In almost any activity, timing is everything. Negotiating before you've found out enough about the job and before the interviewer has found out about how you can be a real value to the company won't work. Delay, delay, delay.

6. **Lacking support for higher pay:** If you're going to ask for more, you better be ready to show the interviewer you're worth more. Present concrete and measurable examples of how you will increase your value by doing more than just your job, making the company money, saving the company money and time, or solving problems on the job.

7. **Forgetting that salary negotiation is different from any other type of negotiation:** After negotiating the price of a car or a home, you'll probably never come into contact with the person with whom you negotiated again. This isn't true with salary and compensation negotiation. You'll most likely see the person you're negotiating with every day that you're working for that company. So be nice to them and make sure they feel like the extra money they invested in you is worth it.

8. **Only negotiating for money:** Sometimes a company can't give you any more money. If you can't get money, you should negotiate for things that translate into money or that make your life easier such as extra vacation time; educational reimbursements; flexible schedules; help in buying tools, computers, or software; travel allowances; and so on.

9. **Getting greedy:** Don't strike a deal and then try to get more when you next see the interviewer. Asking for more after you've struck a verbal agreement just points out that your word isn't worth very much.

10. **Not practicing answers to pay-expectation questions:** You need to make a decision about the types of strategies you're going to use to delay answering interview questions about pay, determine how you are going to address the issue of past salary history and salary

expectations on application forms, and determine when it's time to walk away from the negotiations.

This chapter shows you how to avoid these mistakes and prepares you to answer pay-expectations questions—without putting your foot in your mouth.

How to Delay Discussion of Pay Until It Matters

Many job seekers mishandle discussions of pay early in the interview process. They might not even realize that their responses eliminated them from further consideration. That is why you should avoid discussing compensation if at all possible until a firm job offer is made. Later in this chapter, I'll cover what to do when a job offer is made. But, for now, it is important that you understand that discussing pay before a job offer is made is a trap that can easily result in your being eliminated from consideration.

Let's say that you want to earn about $25,000 a year. An employer asks what your salary requirements are early in the interview, and you tell him or her $25,000. However, the organization wants to pay about $23,000 for that position. The interviewer decides to keep looking for someone who would be delighted with the $23,000 the organization wants to pay.

Had you handled things differently and not "shown your hand," you might have continued a pleasant chat, and the interviewer would have gotten to know you as the wonderful person you are. She or he just might have been able to come up with a few thousand more after having discovered you were worth it.

To avoid losing the job before the interview has really even begun, say that you would be happy to get more specific about salary later, after you have both gotten to know each other better. Only later, when employers want you, are wages an appropriate topic. Remember that a discussion of salary is not necessarily a job offer. More often, it is an attempt to screen you out of consideration. You should never discuss money until the employer indicates he or she wants to offer you a job.

Only Talk Money with the Money People

Never, ever mention a dollar figure until you are sure you're talking to the decision-maker and not a go-between. Usually only the person you will work for directly has the power to accept or reject your requests and make counteroffers. Be assured that interviewers will attempt to wrangle salary information from you early in the screening process. The question often is phrased in a casual tone and comes in many forms. A pressured candidate's natural response to any direct question is to volunteer information (in this case, a dollar figure). Instead, learn to deflect the question to the appropriate person. This process goes something like this:

> **Interviewer:** I'd like to get an idea of your pay expectations. Can you give me a figure?

> **You:** Are you the person who has the power to negotiate my compensation and make the final hiring decision?

> **Interviewer:** No, that would be the hiring manager.

> **You:** Then I would respectfully prefer to wait until I meet with the hiring manager to discuss salary.

What Is Your Current Compensation?

Tom Jackson, author of *Interview Express*, offers this reply: "In my last job, I was paid below the market price for my skills. I was willing to accept this for a while because it gave me the opportunity to learn and develop. Now I am very clear about the value I can offer to an employer and I want my salary to be competitive."

If you feel this type of answer does not reflect your situation, smile and politely reply, "I didn't realize we were ready to discuss salary so soon. I'd feel more comfortable tabling this subject until we are both sure we have a fit."

Another effective tactic is to offer a future-oriented salary figure. The conversation would run something like this: "The job you have described, if carried out in a superior manner, should be worth about $30,000 in three or four years." Most employers don't hesitate to agree because you are talking about a time in the future to work up to that figure. After you reach an agreement, say, "Because we agree that the job will be worth $30,000 in three or four years, I'm content to leave the starting salary up to you.

What do you think would be a reasonable figure?" This approach helps you in a number of ways:

- It indicates that you plan to stay with the company.

- It hints at your willingness to do more than just the job.

- It shows a desire to do quality work.

- It points out your personal motivation to advance.

All of these are traits employers desire.

What Are Your Salary Requirements?

Delay, delay, delay. Doug Matthews of Right Management recommends replying, "Compensation is an important issue. However, my goal is to explore positions that allow me to maximize my strengths and solve significant challenges within an organization. I'm looking for a strong fit between my skills and specific company needs. When that happens, I'm certain the compensation issue will fall into place. Could you give me an idea of the range you've established for this position?"

If the interviewer provides a range, remain quiet for a few seconds. Then say that the upper end of the range is in your ballpark and that you would like to learn more about the position's responsibilities. Notice that you did not agree to anything.

Should the interviewer push for salary requirements, Matthews advises parrying, "I understand the need to discuss specific compensation requirements. However, it might be more effective for me to know how your organization values this position. I'm certain you have ranges for various levels within the organization that are fair, based on experience, responsibility, and contribution. I'd be pleased to work within those ranges. If this is a new position, I'd like to discuss your needs further. Then I might be able to provide a proposal that would help us arrive at an appropriate compensation figure."

Yes, that answer is a mouthful. If you believe that type of answer is too complex for your needs, simply say, "I hesitate to disclose compensation figures because this position contains elements that might differ from my recent position. We might be comparing apples and oranges. Let's table this subject until we're both more comfortable with making an employment offer."

How Much Do You Need to Live On?

If you answer this question in an interview, you probably shouldn't be let out past dark without adult supervision. This appears to be such an innocent and caring question on the surface. Don't be fooled: A literal answer is not in your best interest, as it takes the focus away from how much you are worth and concentrates instead on whether you could do better with your finances. Unfortunately, some employers will use any information you provide to your disadvantage. So, if you're hit with this question, respond by saying something like this:

> *Naturally I've developed a budget for my household, and I'm certainly willing to entertain any offer that covers those expenses. Can you tell me what pay range you have budgeted for this position?*

Online Salary Negotiation Help

You have that job offer in hand—now how can you be sure that you negotiate the salary you deserve? Get inside information and tips at Quintessential Careers' Salary Negotiation Tutorial (www.quintcareers.com/salary_negotiation.html). You'll find tips on getting the best possible salary, turning unacceptable offers into acceptable ones, handling salary discussions during an interview, and more. You'll also find useful articles on negotiation techniques. You can take an online quiz to see how your negotiating techniques stack up and follow links to other salary-negotiation guides.

Job seekers who press for more money based on their personal needs or wants rather than their value to an employer often create bad impressions. The employer might think "Why should I believe that you are responsible and stable if you have financial problems of your own making?" or "My dream of traveling Europe is just as important as your desire to buy a fishing boat." The most sensitive employers might try to help you find ways to reduce your living expenses by suggesting cheaper restaurants, lower-rent apartments, loan-consolidation services, and so on. Remember, you are dealing with a virtual stranger, and asking this person to sympathize with your personal value judgments is completely inappropriate.

Four Rules of Salary Negotiation

To help you avoid making the mistakes we just reviewed, we've developed four basic rules for salary negotiation that you should keep in mind.

Rule #1: Talk Money Only After an Employer Wants You

In the traditional screening process, employers want to know before the interview how much you expect to be paid. They might ask for this information on applications or during a phone screen.

Just why is this information so important to them? Two reasons:

- Employers want to narrow down the field by screening out applicants based solely on pay expectations. This is a critical mistake for interviewers because applicants might have skill sets that genuinely warrant higher pay.

- Employers know that people with high pay expectations who take lower-paying jobs are often dissatisfied with those jobs and leave for better-paying jobs as soon as possible.

Delay, Delay, Delay!

Every career pro in the world will tell you to use a stalling strategy and not give a specific dollar amount when asked about pay expectations until a job offer is tendered. So you should try to defer salary questions until you are sure it's the real thing and not just part of a screening process. Then, when the timing is right, maneuver the interviewer into naming the starting point. The rationale behind the stalling strategy is that if you come in too high, or too low, you might be eliminated from consideration. Always remember the two most important rules of salary negotiations: "Almost everything is negotiable; and those who talk money first usually lose."

Why Delaying Tactics Work to Your Advantage

There are three primary reasons why delaying your answer to pay expectation questions works to your advantage:

- You have the chance to gather more information about the job and then discuss how what you've learned about the job can enhance your value to the company.

- The more time you can spend talking about your skills, abilities, and experiences, the more value you will generate in the interviewer's mind.

- The more time, psychological energy, and effort an employer invests learning about you through interviewing, reference checking, abilities testing, drug testing, checking school records, and so on, the less likely the employer will risk losing you just because of a few extra dollars.

In figure 8.1, you can see how the flow of negotiation power shifts from the interviewer to the interviewee as he or she goes through different interview phases.

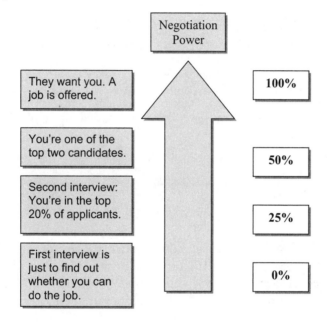

Figure 8.1: Negotiation power.

As you can see, discussing salary early in the interviewing process is not to your advantage. Your best position is to use techniques that are likely to satisfy a curious employer without giving a specific dollar amount. The following are a few ways you could respond to an initial interview inquiry about your pay expectations:

- "What salary range do you pay for positions with similar requirements?"

- "I'm very interested in the position, and my salary would be negotiable."

- "Tell me what you have in mind for the salary range."

- "I am interested in the job and would consider any reasonable offer you might make."

According to outplacement industry surveys, salary issues are one of the main reasons candidates are knocked out of the running during the screening process. Responding appropriately to salary questions can get you past screening interviewers, who rarely have authority to negotiate salaries, and in front of decision-makers with whom the real negotiations take place.

Two More Rules of Delaying

1. Always give the interviewer a pertinent reason for delaying the discussion of pay, benefit, and perks (such as wanting to make certain the position is an exact fit for the salary range you were considering or that you want to be certain your talents have been completely presented so that an accurate price for them can be named). This prevents you from honking the interviewer off with your approach.

2. Always try to find out more about the demands of the job and what the interviewer considers an ideal candidate when you're in delay mode. You can use this information to support a higher starting pay rate.

With a bit of luck, stall tactics such as these will get the employer to tell you the salary range or at least delay further discussion until later, when it matters. If these tactics don't work and the employer still insists on knowing your salary expectations, there are more things you can do.

Rule #2: Know the Probable Salary Range in Advance

Approaching an interview without being prepared for discussions of pay is not wise. Although you will have to do a bit of research, knowing what an employer is likely to pay is essential in salary negotiations.

The trick is to think in terms of a *range* in salaries, rather than a particular number. Keep in mind that larger organizations tend to pay more than smaller ones, and various areas of the country differ greatly in pay scales. Find out the general range that jobs of this sort are likely to pay in your area. That information is relatively easy to obtain; all it takes is asking those who work in similar jobs, finding the information online, or visiting the library. See "Sources of Information on Salary and Wages" at the end of this chapter for tips on finding this information.

A couple of cautions are in order here:

- Salaries and compensation packages, like politics, tend to be local. So if you're using national averages, you could be wide or short of the mark. You should find out the low, the high, and the average salary and compensation levels for someone with your level of skills, experience, and education in the geographical areas to which you're applying.

- If you tell an interviewer that you've researched the local labor market, you better have copies of your sources with you, just in case the interviewer challenges your information's credibility.

Rule #3: Bracket the Salary Range

Salary bracketing is a proven method of dealing with pay expectation questions. There are three types of brackets you might want to consider using: the low bracket, the mid-range bracket, and the high bracket.

The Low Bracket

If the employer says the salary range is between $26,000 and $30,000, and your research shows this to be a reasonable range, you might respond by saying something like this:

From the salary and compensation research I've done, that is a fair range. Is it okay to hold off on my setting a specific dollar amount until I find out more about the job demands and you find out more about what I can bring to the company?

By using this approach, you agree to the employer's range but still have $4,000 of wiggle room to increase your starting pay. And you delay your commitment to a specific dollar amount.

The Mid-range Bracket

If the employer says the salary range is between $26,000 and $30,000, you might respond by saying something like this:

From the salary and compensation research I've done, the average pay ranges from $28,000 to $32,000 for a person with my experience. If this range is acceptable, can we talk money specifics later, when I know more about the job and your expectations?

This approach splits the employer's bracket in half with your low side falling within the employer's range but your high side above it. You get a little more negotiation room and the employer doesn't have to commit to the higher price for your services and skills.

The High Bracket

If the employer says the salary range is between $26,000 and $30,000, you might respond by saying something like this:

$30,000 to $34,000 is the range I had in mind, so it seems like we're in the ballpark with each other.

If the employer doesn't balk, you know you're in good shape. By using this approach, you still touch on one side of the employer's range, leaving negotiation room for both you and the employer.

Talking in terms of a salary range that extends a bit above what the employer offered can result in one of two positive outcomes:

- If offered the job, you are likely to be offered more than the employer originally considered.

- It gives you the option of negotiating your salary above the original range offered while still keeping yourself in the running by touching on that range.

Rule #4: Don't Say No Too Soon

Too often, people lose the ability to negotiate salary because they mishandle the actual job offer. This brings us to rule #4: Never say no to a job offer either before it is made or within 24 hours after.

First, you need some time to think about whether you really want the job. You also need to do more research on whether the offer is appropriate for the job. But also, if the employer senses that you might not accept, he might be able to come up with more money before you talk again. See "The Offer Is Not What You Want" later in this chapter for a script for handling this situation.

What to Say When an Offer Is Made

Serious negotiation often begins only after you've been invited to several interviews—but not always. When employers are ready to make an offer, they come right out and say, "We'd like to offer you the position, provided we can come to an agreement on compensation." Again, let the employer open up the bidding. The employer is likely to make a very low offer or a reasonable one. The following sections explain what you should say in each situation.

The Offer Is Not What You Want

At the point in time when the employer is offering you the job, you need to keep rule #4 in mind. Never say no to a job offer either before it is made or within 24 hours afterward!

Let's say that you get a job offer at half the salary you expected. Avoid the temptation to turn it down there and then. Instead, say something like this:

> *Thank you for your offer. I am flattered that you think I am the right person for the job. Because this decision is so important to me, I would like to consider your offer and get back with you within two days.*

Leave and see if you change your mind. If not, call back and say something like this:

> *I've given your offer considerable thought and feel that I just can't take it at the salary you've offered. Is there any way you can help me figure out how I can be paid in the range of _____?*

Even as you say no, leave the door open to keep negotiating. If the employer wants you, he or she might be willing to meet your terms. It happens more than you might imagine. If the employer cannot meet your salary needs, say thank you again, and let him or her know you are interested in future openings within your salary range. Then, stay in touch.

> **Tip:** *Do not reject a job offer to try to get a higher wage. Understand that once you reject an offer, the deal is off. You lose that job forever.*

The Offer Is Reasonable

Just as you shouldn't reject an offer too quickly, take time in accepting a job, too. Accepting a reasonable offer right away can be a mistake. At the very least a job offer should include information on the following:

- Position title
- Position responsibilities

- Starting salary
- Benefits and perquisites
- Starting dates
- Working location(s)
- Incentives and bonuses
- Reporting relationships
- Performance review timelines
- Advancement and raises
- Special agreements
- Other duties that might be assigned

If you don't have the preceding information yet, don't make a move you could regret. Instead, keep plugging away until the picture comes into clear focus.

Also, discussing the offer with others before saying yes is often wise. Here is one way to delay until you can give the offer some thought:

Thank you for the offer. The position is very much what I wanted in many ways, and I am delighted with your interest. This decision is an important one for me, and I would like some time to consider your offer.

Ask for 24 hours to consider your decision and, when calling back, consider negotiating for something reasonable. A bit more money, every other Tuesday afternoon off, or some other benefit would be nice if you can get it easily. However, if you want the job, do not jeopardize obtaining it with unreasonable demands. If your request causes a problem, make it very clear that you want the job anyway.

They Offer, You Want It—Now It's Time to Negotiate!

The employer you've spent the past two weeks wooing has opened the bidding with a lukewarm figure below what you feel you are worth. But exactly how should you ask for more? You aren't a professional athlete with a savvy manager to wheel and deal the details, and isn't the time limit on this opportunity short?

Know Your Price

Once you've reached this stage of the game, you should be in tune with industry standards and local pay ranges and have correctly "encouraged" the interviewer to name the opening dollar figure. Know your worst-case pay and your best possible result. You come up with these numbers through your research on the industry and a serious study of your personal financial position. Plan to start the bidding at your best possible result. Should the offer fail to rise above your worst-case pay, continue job hunting.

> **Tip:** *Always heed the advice Tom Jackson dishes out in* Interview Express: *Negotiations should never be angry or emotional, no matter how much pressure there is on either side. Assert your value so that the employer will view you as a highly worthwhile addition rather than as someone who is overpriced.*

Playing the Negotiation Game

There are a few negotiation rules of the road you should pay attention to:

- Be ready to provide rationale for deserving higher pay or whatever it is that is stopping you from accepting the offer (relocation, shift schedule, and so on).

- Don't make demands, present ultimatums, or threaten to work for a competitor. If you do, you're not negotiating.

- Use tact, style, and class. Try to see things from the negotiator's point of view. Remember what your mom said about it being easier to catch flies with honey than with vinegar.

- Don't try to negotiate everything. Identify one, two, or three elements you want to improve.

- Don't negotiate more than one element at a time. If it's vacation, deal with only that before moving to the next point.

- Prioritize your needs, wants, and desires.

- Determine what you're willing to give up to get what you need.

- Keep letting interviewers know you want to work there, provided a deal can be struck.

If the offer tendered isn't what you're willing to accept, one of your best strategies is to smile, shake your head, and then shut up. Remember how employers use silence to get more information from you during the interview? Well turnabout is fair play and often results in the employer real-izing that something is wrong with the offer. At this point he or she will most likely ask you about your concerns, putting you in the driver's seat.

Career consultants Haldane Associates discovered that in more than 50 per-cent of all situations where silence is used, the interviewers cough up a higher figure without further discussion! However, when a better offer isn't immediately presented in response to your silence, one of two other things will happen. The interviewer will either explain the offer or ask you for your reaction. In the first instance, listen politely but continue your thoughtful silence as long as necessary. In the latter case, indicate that you are enthusiastic about the job, but the offer is on the modest side. Then suggest continuing the discussion at another meeting—the following day, if possible.

Unfortunately many job candidates interpret this tactic as "playing hard to get." Haldane Associates scoffs at this label, and so should you. In fact, this consulting firm has interviewed a number of employers who stated that employees who handled themselves well during their salary negotiations were treated with greater respect and given more opportunities to advance within the organization.

Ending the Negotiation

Several clues tip you off to the fact that the employer has extended its best possible salary package. If the same figure is repeated after a day or two break, chances are good it won't change. Perhaps the employer has started tossing in additional benefits without changing the figure, again signaling that the price is firm.

Once your salary has been decided, begin hashing out these areas:

- Stock options

- Vacation time

- Performance bonuses

- Flexible time (for example, working four 10-hour days and take Fridays off; working 10 a.m. to 6:00 p.m. to avoid rush hours; job-sharing; telecommuting)

- Parking privileges

Tip: *Whether or not you are satisfied with the salary eventually settled upon, don't forget Haldane Associates' most valu-able advice: Always ask for a commitment to review your salary in six months, based on your demonstrated value.*

- Company car

- Geographic location, if there is more than one office

Before you shake hands to seal the deal, ask for 24 hours to think it over. Such careful thought and responsible consideration can only be viewed as professional and will earn the respect of a potential employer.

Get the Job Offer in Writing

You're not in Judge Judy's court where verbal agreements can be litigated. You're in the labor market—and there's lots of miscommunication. Ask the person making the offer to put it down on paper. Let the person know it's not that you distrust them, but that you fear what would happen if he or she got hit by a car while leaving work. You can also tell the interviewer that you don't want to forget anything or have any misunderstandings after you begin the job. If the person offering you the job refuses to put it in writing, ask yourself if the person is being upfront and honest with his or her portrayal of your pay, duties, work settings, environment, and so on.

> **Note:** *According to the International Association of Corporate and Professional Recruiters, Inc., financial incentives, equity opportunity, and geographic location rank as the top three motivating factors respectively in evaluating a job offer. Time flexibility, health insurance policies, and maternal/paternal leave policies ranked fourth through sixth.*

"Other Duties As Assigned"

You wouldn't sign a car loan agreement that had the phrase "and other payments as assigned," would you? You shouldn't blindly accept such a phrase when accepting a job offer either. Anytime you see or hear the phrase "other duties as assigned," it's a good idea to try to find out just what those duties are. Those "other duties" might change the whole dynamic of the job you think you're going to perform. Or those "other duties" might use skill sets that make you a more valuable employee and should result in higher pay.

Sources of Information on Salary and Wages

You have already learned a variety of good techniques for negotiating your pay, but their effective use requires that you know in advance the prevailing pay scale for the jobs you want. Although you often won't know precisely how much a particular employer might pay, some quick research can give you a good idea.

When asked to relate the number-one mistake job candidates make during the negotiation process, most employers say it is a failure to prepare. For those job seekers who take the time and effort to investigate salary ranges and benefits rather than simply "winging it," the rewards are worth every second of research.

Like other parts of the job search process, the key to salary negotiations is preparation. It is very important for you to do your research before you begin negotiations. In order to determine the salary you are willing to accept, investigate the salary range someone with your skills and experience can expect to receive. This section gives you a handle on where to locate such information quickly.

The Internet

Use the sites in this section to learn the average pay rates in your chosen field and find cost-of-living information for different parts of the country.

- **BankRate Cost of Living Comparison Calculator (www.bankrate.com/brm/movecalc.asp):** Thinking about relocating for a job? Compare the cost of living among hundreds of U.S. with this handy salary calculator. Just enter your salary and current location, and then select another city to find out what you'll need to make there to sustain the same standard of living.

- **JobStar Salary Information (http://jobstar.org/tools/salary/):** You can jump directly to JobStar's more than 300 links to general and profession-specific salary surveys and also take some time to explore salary negotiation strategies and test your own salary IQ. Information on print resources you might want to check out is also included. The site links to California libraries, but you can look up these books in your own public library.

- **PayScale.com (www.payscale.com):** This up-and-coming site enables you to generate a free personal salary profile tailored to the job you seek. You can also use the site's free tools and calculators to help you make the best negotiation decisions.

- **Salary.com (www.salary.com):** Use the Salary Wizard tool to get a quick, free base salary range for your job. More detailed reports are available for purchase. Employers can also use this site to research salary ranges for open positions.

- **Salary Expert (www.salaryexpert.com):** Find free basic regional salary reports by selecting your job title and then your ZIP code or city. Reports list the position's average salary, benefits, and bonuses; show how salaries in a given area compare to the national average; provide a brief description of the occupation; give the average cost of living in the area; and list links to salary info for related jobs. Also available at this site are selected feature articles and international salary reports.

Reference Books

Your local library or bookstore should have a number of references to help you determine the salary range for the occupation you are considering. A list of such references follows. Ask your librarian for assistance because most libraries provide a variety of references that might not be listed here.

- *Salary Facts Handbook* (JIST Works)

- The *Occupational Outlook Handbook* (JIST Works)

- *College Majors Handbook with Real Career Paths and Payoffs* (JIST Works)

- *Best Jobs for the 21st Century* (JIST Works)

- *American Salaries and Wages Survey* (Gale Group)

Professional Associations

Virtually every occupation and industry you can imagine (and some that you can't) has one or more associations. Most of the larger ones conduct salary surveys on an annual basis. This information is available to members and, sometimes, in their publications. Back issues of an association's journals or newsletters (if you can get them) can provide excellent information on trends, including pay rates. Consider joining an association to get access to this information, as well as access to local members with whom you can network. You can search for associations by industry and geographic location at the American Society of Association Executives Web site at www.asaecenter.org/Directories/AssociationSearch.cfm.

Local Information

Local pay rates can differ substantially from national averages; starting wages are often substantially less than those for experienced workers; some industries pay better than others; and smaller organizations often pay less than larger ones. For these reasons, you need to find out prevailing pay rates for jobs similar to those you seek. Following are some additional sources of this information:

- **Your network:** Talk to colleagues. Although people frequently don't want to tell you what they personally are making, usually they are willing to talk about salary ranges. Ask colleagues, based on their experience, what salary range you might expect for the position.

- **Job search centers:** These centers (which you can find in schools, libraries, and community centers or as part of federal, state, or local government programs) frequently keep salary information on hand.

- **Your past experience:** If you are applying for a job in a field in which you have experience, you probably have a good idea of what someone with your skills and abilities should be paid. Think about your past salary. Unless the job you are applying for requires a dramatically different amount of responsibility than your former position, your previous salary is definitely a starting point for negotiations.

Key Points: Chapter 8

- Avoid discussing salary until after an employer offers you a job. If the employer insists on having a number, offer a salary range.

- Don't accept or reject a job offer right away. Take two days to think about it, and make sure you have the information you need to make your decision.

- Let the employer name a salary first, and then you can negotiate up from there.

- Prepare yourself for salary discussions by researching salaries for the position you are applying for. Be sure to find as much local information as possible because pay varies widely depending on location.

Online Interviewing Resources

The Internet has a wealth of information that you can use to support your interviewing and job search efforts. Here are some of the most helpful sites I've found.

Interviewing Tips

Equal Employment Opportunity Commission (EEOC)
www.eeoc.gov

Interviewing Success
www.collegegrad.com/intv/

Job-Interview.net
www.job-interview.net

Monster: Interview Center
http://interview.monster.com

Quintessential Careers: Job Interviewing Resources
www.quintcareers.com/intvres.html

Informational Interviews

Quintessential Careers: Informational Interviewing Tutorial
www.quintcareers.com/informational_interviewing.html

Job and Industry Information

Career Guide to Industries
http://stats.bls.gov/oco/cg/home.htm

Hoover's Online
www.hoovers.com

JIST Publishing
www.jist.com

Occupational Outlook Handbook
www.bls.gov/oco/

Occupational Information Network (O*NET)
http://online.onetcenter.org

Company Information

CorporateInformation.com
www.corporateinformation.com

Google News
http://news.google.com

Industry Research Desk
www.virtualpet.com/industry/

Riley Guide: Using the Internet to Do Job Search Research
www.rileyguide.com/jsresearch.html

Search Engine Showdown
http://www.searchengineshowdown.com

SuperPages
www.superpages.com/business/

Thomas Register
www.thomasnet.com

Yahoo! News
http://news.yahoo.com

Researching and Negotiating Salaries

Abbott, Langer & Associates
www.abbott-langer.com

America's Career InfoNet
www.acinet.org/acinet/

JobStar Salary Information
http://jobstar.org/tools/salary/

Quintessential Careers' salary-negotiation tutorial
www.quintcareers.com/salary_negotiation.html

The Salary Calculator
www.homefair.com/calc/salcalc.html

Salary Expert
www.salaryexpert.com

Finding and Applying for Job Openings

America's Job Bank (AJB)
www.jobbankinfo.org

BestJobsUSA.com
www.bestjobsusa.com

CareerBuilder.com
www.careerbuilder.com

Careerbuzz
www.careerbuzz.com

CareerSite
www.careersite.com

FlipDog.com
http://flipdog.com

JobBankUSA.com
www.jobbankusa.com

Monster
www.monster.com

NationJob
www.nationjob.com

Vault.com
www.vault.com

Yahoo! HotJobs
http://hotjobs.yahoo.com

Index